PAINTING BUILDINGS IN WATERCOLOR

PAINTING BUILDINGS IN WATERCOLOR
By Arthur J. Barbour

WATSON-GUPTILL PUBLICATIONS/NEW YORK

PITMAN PUBLISHING/LONDON

First published 1973 in the United States and Canada by Watson-Guptill Publications,
a division of Billboard Publications, Inc.,
165 West 46 Street, New York, N.Y.

Published simultaneously in Great Britain by Sir Isaac Pitman & Sons Ltd.,
39 Parker Street, Kingsway, London WC2B 5PB
(U.K.) ISBN 0-273-00261-9

Manufactured in Japan

Library of Congress Cataloging in Publication Data
Barbour, Arthur J 1926–
    Painting buildings in watercolor.
    Bibliography: p.
    1. Buildings in art.   2. Water-color painting—
Technique.   I.   Title.
ND2310.B37   751.4′22   72-12765
ISBN 0-8230-3583-2
First Printing, 1973

This book is dedicated to "MARY" for her unfailing help.

ACKNOWLEDGMENTS

I would like to thank the following people for their contributions to this book:

Bernard Guerlain of Special Papers, Inc., West Redding, Connecticut, for his special technical knowledge regarding the Arches watercolor papers that I used for all the demonstrations in this book.

Alfred Latini of Paterson, New Jersey, for his constructive criticism of the chapter on Materials and Tools, as well as for his photographs which appear on pages 131 and 134 in the chapter entitled *Some Problems and How to Correct Them.*

Stan Hufschmidt of West Milford, New Jersey, for his photographic advice and for the biographical photograph which appears on the back flap of the jacket. Norman Morse of Ringwood, New Jersey, for his deft photographic advice. Robert Gibson of Ringwood, New Jersey, for the photographs which appear on pages 130 and 135 of the chapter entitled *Some Problems and How to Correct Them.*

The Ford Motor Company for permission to reproduce *Vizcaya,* which is in their permanent collection.

Nancy Levine of Ringwood, New Jersey, for typing portions of the manuscript. Donald Holden of Watson-Guptill Publications for helping to make this book possible. Lois Miller of Watson-Guptill Publications for editing this book.

My parents, Dr. and Mrs. Peter J. Barbour, for their contribution to this book, and my wife Margie for her constant support and thoughtfulness and for her careful attention to the typing of the manuscript.

CONTENTS

INTRODUCTION

The main purpose of this book is to give you, its reader, all the knowledge of materials and techniques required to render buildings in a realistic manner. I've tried to accomplish this by working forward, not backward, recording each painting photographically in a step-by-step procedure.

I've used as many as 15 steps in some demonstrations to bring a painting to its conclusion. All the demonstrations are authentic happenings. Every step is recorded as it took place, with all the mistakes—and the methods of correcting them—here for you to see and study.

I put these watercolors together in a period of 18 months, painting each one before the camera. I've packed this book with information that will help the beginner, and I've also geared the demonstrations to the artist who is trying to achieve that one step beyond the basics.

Other artists may have secrets they withhold, but I certainly do not. Within the scope of this book, I've tried to present every important secret—and all the painting know-how—that I've acquired in 25 years of thinking, studying, and pondering about the best way to paint a picture that's fun and yet challenging, abstract in its parts and pieces and yet realistic in its completed form.

My palette is simple, with few colors, yet each of my paintings has its own unique color scheme. I'll show you how to achieve this variety, as well as how to mix color, use ink with color, and apply color with brushes and other materials; how to run washes, paint dry-brush, and paint wet-in-wet; how to stipple, spatter, scrub out, lift out, sponge out, alter unacceptable passages, and repaint them in a more pleasing form; how to deepen existing washes; how to create effects and moods with color; how to paint buildings in shadow, and sunlight on buildings; and how to render intricate detail simply.

I hope you'll learn all these things as you read and follow the step-by-step demonstrations in this book, as well as how to paint surrounding landscapes, skies, trees, bushes, mountains, foregrounds, rocks, and water. Along with all these techniques and procedures, I've tried to give you as many little insights into painting as I can impart in one book.

There is also a special, illustrated chapter in the back of the book describing many of the problems that can arise in the course of completing a painting—and how to resolve them. Here, you'll see what measures an artist will take to rescue a picture that might otherwise be a lost cause.

I think this book will be a valuable addition to the studio or bookshelf of the beginning and advanced watercolor student alike. I've tried to make it an adventure in watercolor, showing the pitfalls and aggravations that can confront a painter—and describing the techniques that can lead him to success.

MATERIALS AND TOOLS

Let's start with a brief review of the wide range of materials and tools you'll eventually want to have at your disposal. As you progress, experiment with as many of these as you can—so you can see for yourself the part each one plays in creating the textures and effects you're after.

Paper

The relative weight of a particular watercolor paper is expressed in pounds per ream: a ream contains 500 sheets. For example, a sheet of 300 lb. paper does *not* weigh 300 lbs. itself, but a *ream* of it does weigh 300 lb. Similarly, 500 sheets of 140 lb. paper weigh 140 lb. The standard, so-called Imperial size sheet is 22" x 30". Watercolor paper is also available commercially mounted on board, in the standard sizes.

Even when you use the same brand of paper and the same surface, different weights will produce different effects in your painting. There are many things you have to investigate for yourself in watercolor painting, and this is one of them. These differences are so subtle that they must be experienced firsthand. For example, observe the subtle differences in the way washes will dry on various weights of paper.

Watercolor paper comes in three surfaces: *hot-pressed*, which means very smooth; *cold-pressed*, which means moderately textured; and *rough*, which means coarsely textured. The surface of a paper has a lot to do with how a wash will behave when it first goes on, when it settles into the paper, and when it dries. You can use the surface of a paper to achieve various color and textural effects. A very smooth, hot-pressed paper will produce a more intense hue than a very rough-surfaced watercolor paper. The smooth surface reflects the light directly back to the eye, whereas the irregular bumps on rough paper diffuse the reflected light and soften the brilliance of the color. It is the light reflected from the white surface of the paper—through the transparent color—that gives watercolor paintings their brilliance.

The smoother the paper, the more you can see the sedimentation of the color pigments of a wet wash as they gently settle to the surface in an irregular, enhancing design of their own. On a rough paper, this sedimentation is not nearly as noticeable; but the rough paper lends its own irregular texture to the washes.

Until now, I've been speaking of smooth (hot-pressed) paper and rough paper. Now, for a paper between these two textures, called *cold-pressed*. The texture of cold-pressed paper is not too smooth and not too rough. It has a little of the rough texture that is good for drybrush and a little of the smooth texture that shows the sedimentation of pigment. This is the paper I have preferred for many years and have worked on primarily. The cold-pressed 300 lb. Arches paper has the weight and texture I've selected for most of the full-color paintings and for the black-and-white works which appear in this book.

Selecting Colors

The palette I use consists primarily of pigment colors, with a few dye colors. Pigments are color particles that are made of finely ground, granular substances. These particles are deposited on the surface of the paper and can be sponged off the paper rather easily, leaving the surface almost white. Dye colors, on the other hand, are *not* finely ground particles, but organic and inorganic liquids that penetrate and stain the very fibers of the paper. Thus, dye colors are difficult to remove. If you try to remove a mixture of pigment and dye colors from your paper, the pigment colors will wash away and the dye colors will leave a strong stain that is virtually impossible to sponge out completely.

Earth colors—like raw and burnt umber and raw and burnt sienna—are pigment colors made from natural deposits of ores and minerals. Cobalt and ultramarine blue are pigment colors too. Alizarin crimson is a typical dye color.

The following are the colors I have on my palette

and recommend to you. They're all available in tubes, and are moist and ready to use.

burnt sienna
burnt umber
raw sienna
raw umber
cobalt blue
ultramarine blue
permanent blue
sap green
cadmium orange
cadmium yellow medium
cadmium red
alizarin crimson
black India ink (Higgins)

How Colors Behave

Here's a brief explanation of the way these colors behave when I use them. Of course, you should experiment with them and observe their characteristics for yourself. Choice of color is personal, and you may well develop a palette that differs from mine.

Burnt Sienna. One of my favorites. It has a rich, rust-brown hue. You can use it to mix beautiful grays by introducing varying quantities of it into blue mixtures. It will be a warmer mixture if the burnt sienna is dominant, a cooler mixture if the blue is dominant. Gray mixtures also vary in color depending on which blue you use, and you should definitely investigate these differences thoroughly. As you'll see in later demonstrations, burnt sienna is a great color to "squish" into areas of solid green foliage to break up the monotony of the green and create color variety. I also use it for just what it looks like—rust stains!

Burnt Umber. Deeper in value and not as brilliant as burnt sienna. Burnt umber, mixed with cobalt, ultramarine, or permanent blue, gives a lower-key, subtler hue to gray mixtures. Burnt umber mixed with cobalt blue, for instance, produces a silvery gray, while burnt umber mixed with ultramarine blue produces a more transparent, granular effect. Investigate and study these mixtures until they become part of your painting vocabulary.

Raw Sienna. A yellowish, tannish, golden color, a little cooler and more transparent than yellow ochre. It gives a soft, greenish hue when it's mixed with blue, and a little touch of sap green in this mixture will give you a nice spring green that's not too sharp. I use various mixtures of these colors for practically all my greens. You can use raw sienna as a sky wash, either by itself or mixed with such warm colors as burnt sienna and cadmium red.

Raw Umber. A rather muted, yellowish-brown hue, a little cooler than burnt umber. It also creates greenish-blue hues when it's mixed with blue. It can be used in sky washes, foliage, and foregrounds; and it makes a good, low-keyed green for grass when it's

mixed with sap green. It's good for modifying shrub, brush, and scrub areas.

Cobalt Blue. Of all the blues, the one I use most often. It's a soft, velvety blue with a tinge of green, and it mixes well with earth colors. I use this 75% of the time in sky washes, sometimes mixed with permanent blue to give a greenish cast, but usually by itself. Mixed with cadmium red, it produces a beautiful bluish-purple color for indicating cast shadows on white buildings.

Ultramarine Blue. A purplish blue, more grainy than cobalt, with a sharper hue. Mixed with burnt sienna, it gives a lovely granular effect when it settles onto the paper surface in wet washes. It can be used in sky washes, cast shadows, and purple mountains, and it mixes well with all colors.

Sap Green. A slightly yellowish green dye color that stains the paper. It mixes well with earth colors, making beautiful greens when mixed with raw sienna and blue, or simply with raw sienna or raw umber. I depend heavily on sap green, although it's not as light-fast as more permanent colors.

Cadmium Orange. A very warm orange that you should use quite sparingly. It's like all the cadmiums: rather opaque. I use it in about one out of ten paintings, and then I use it instinctively, rather than deliberately. In landscapes—in foliage, buildings, and foregrounds—it gives a lovely, warm summer-evening glow, like sunlight on red cedars near the end of day. It remains quite opaque when it's mixed with other colors.

Cadmium Yellow Medium. Also quite opaque. You can use it by itself for brilliant spots of sunlit color such as those found on clothing, mixed with green for spring grass, and mixed with black watercolor for a beautiful, low-key olive green.

Cadmium Red. The only red I use. It has a slightly orange cast and is also quite opaque. I use it often mixed with other colors, such as raw sienna and burnt sienna, as a pale sky wash, before I introduce stronger mixtures of gray and other colors.

Alizarin Crimson. A very powerful color. Its red cast overpowers any mixture. I seldom use it, unless I want a very strong purplish red accent.

Black India Ink. I sometimes use this heavily, and, on other occasions, I hardly use it at all, depending on the degree of texture and definition I'm trying to achieve. I first started using India ink for pine trees and other foliage, and lately I've been using it to define shadows and textures on buildings. I usually mix it with other colors, or add it to the wet washes of other colors. I prefer it to black watercolor paint because it doesn't spread too far when I add it to wet washes. The ink usually goes into a wet wash, spreads nicely to make a feathery edge, then—unlike paint—it "grabs" the surface of paper and stops spreading. When it's mixed with other colors in wet washes, it also stops those colors from spreading too much.

Brushes

My brushes are almost all sabeline; and, as I literally destroy them with rough handling, I use a cheaper grade, which I find holds up better for my purposes than pure red sable.

In a *round brush,* the hairs are fixed into one end of a cylindrical metal holder (the ferrule), so they form a cylindrical shape and come to a point. Round sable brushes are normally used in the smaller passages of paintings, rarely in large sky washes. But, I must admit that, except for the sky, I use round brushes for just about every part of my paintings.

In a *flat sabeline brush,* the end of the metal ferrule that receives the wooden or plastic handle is round, while the end that holds the hairs is flattened out. Thus, the hairs form a rectangle with a squarish tip. Flat brushes are very handy for applying large washes.

Flat bristle brushes are the same as flat sabeline, except that the bristles are made of hog hair, rather than sable, and are very stiff. I mention this brush here, and I always have it handy, but I don't use it as much as I use the other brushes. It is, however, very useful for lifting out color and for applying color in vertical strokes.

Another brush that I have around, but don't use very often, is a *No. 10 red sable oil brush,* which has shorter hairs than watercolor brushes.

Other Tools

For sponges, I recommend only real or natural sponges, because they're so much softer and easier on the surface of the paper than artificial sponges. Plastic sponges seem to inflict fine scratches on the paper when they're used heavily.

A piece of matchbook cover, or any piece of heavy paper or cardboard, can be used as a "squeegee" to squeeze paint into wet washes and to apply paint dry. Use of a squeegee can give an entirely different look to old buildings, wood fences, sheds, and rock piles. Fold the cardboard once to about 1″ x 2″ to make it sturdy. Then, scoop up undiluted paint or mixtures of pure paint straight from the tube, and "squish" it into either a semi-wet wash or directly onto dry paper.

Knives and razor blades are used primarily for scratching out small effects, such as twigs and branches, or the sunlit edge of a building. Any single-edged blade will do, although I usually prefer an X-Acto knife with a No. 11 blade. Never overdo this effect: use it sparingly.

When a wash is nearly dry—especially a deep, lush wash—you can take the handle of your brush and press the tip into the wash with a short, scraping motion. The pressure will force the moist pigment out of the paper, leaving a light line. This method is good for indicating foliage and accenting twigs and small trees.

Accessories

There is a wide variety of drawing pencils available, but I prefer a regular No. 2 writing pencil because it's dark enough yet soft enough not to hurt the paper and it erases easily.

For erasing, a Staedtler Mars-Plastic eraser goes down into the surface of the paper and removes the soft graphite without hurting the paper. You'll find it more gentle on the surface of your paper than regular art gum. I also use an electric eraser to pick up a highlight here and there, wherever I prefer a soft highlight to the hard-edged highlight the knife blade creates. You can use an electric eraser to erase or burnish out very small areas on buildings, to make a color change, or to correct very small areas that are not working out right. Remember that this, too, can tear through a lighter weight paper, such as 140 lb., and don't overdo your use of it, or the results will become too obvious and will offend the eye.

When I do a straight-on view of a building, I usually use a T-square and triangle to keep things lined up vertically. These make the drawing quite exact and rather tight, but you can then paint it loosely to convey a more casual atmosphere.

For a palette, I've discovered that a large, enamel butcher's tray, something in the neighborhood of 13″ x 19″, fits my purposes best of all. (Several years ago I worked right on top of a white, porcelain-topped kitchen table and found this excellent, too. You can load it up with paint, then wipe it clean with a damp cloth.)

I have no system for laying out my paint. I just squeeze several gobs of paint onto different areas of my butcher's tray. I usually put the blues and browns somewhere near each other, then I place any red or green at the opposite end of the tray—and from then on, I just add paint as I need it, anywhere on the tray.

My working table is a large, wooden 3′ x 5′ office desk. I've also used regular card tables. I work always flat for better control of my washes, and I only elevate my watercolor board as a last resort, to stop a large sky wash from creeping as it dries.

I have two old drawing boards, 31″ x 23″ x 3/4″, that I've used over the years for stretching watercolor paper. I also use 3/4″ plywood cut to 24″ x 32″ for Imperial-size sheets of paper, and some cut to 29″ x 42″ for "double elephant" (27″ x 40″) sheets. I prefer plywood because it will not come apart with heavy usage, as some drawing boards do.

For stretching watercolor paper, I use gummed tape—not sticky masking tape, but the water-soluble kind that's used for sealing cardboard cartons. To stretch your paper, draw a line about 3/8″ to 1/2″ in from the edge, all the way around. Soak this sheet in water for about 20 minutes—use the bathtub. The paper will absorb water as it soaks and will be as much as 3/8″ to 1/2″ larger all around than it was originally. Place your wet sheet on the flat board. I usually put a layer of paper towels between the wet paper and the board, to make the paper a little more resilient for painting. It also helps keep the reverse side clean so that, if you decide not to keep your finished painting, you can turn it over and use the other side.

Now, use paper towels to dry about 2″ of the outer edge of the paper, all the way around. Pat it with a couple of sheets of paper towels until the edges are quite dry to the touch. Now, wet your gummed tape— you may use a sponge for this, or a regular tape machine made for this purpose, or drag the gummed side through a shallow plate filled with water—and glue the watercolor paper right to the board. Run long strips of tape the full length of all four sides of the sheet. Put the inner edge of the moistened gummed tape along the pencil line; the rest of the tape should extend onto the board. Press on the tape several times to make it adhere firmly to both the paper and the board. Let this dry in a flat position overnight, or for several hours, until the paper is completely dry and ready for you to draw and work on. After you've completed the painting, you can remove it from the board by cutting it off at the edges with a sharp razor blade.

I work under artificial fluorescent light, using both cool white and daylight bulbs. This gives me a lighting effect very close to the natural light outside. I've worked with this type of lighting for years, and I have no trouble adjusting to natural daylight when I occasionally work outside.

Once in a while, I use masking tape as friskets when I lift out or sponge out small areas. This is fairly easy to do on a tough-surfaced paper like Arches, and, if I'm careful when I remove the tape, I don't lift the surface of the paper with it at all.

Today, many foods come in plastic containers, and some of these make excellent water containers. Very often, I cut the top off a bleach container to make a large, open container that's easy to work with: in the excitement of painting, I don't miss the opening as I dip the brush into it.

A small metal tool box with a divided top drawer makes a good paintbox. Tubes of watercolor fit easily into the upper divisions, along with razor and X-Acto knife blades, erasers, and matches. The large bottom area can be used for brushes, sponges, pencils, India ink, paper towels, and masking tape.

When I paint "on the spot," I still like to have the comforts of my studio; so I take along a folding card table, at which I stand and paint. If my location is not in the shade, I use a beach umbrella to keep the direct sunlight off the paper.

Try to keep the reflection of white, sunlit paper out of your eyes. If necessary when you're painting in snow or on the beach, use sunglasses to avoid the sun's glare. Surprisingly, you won't have any trouble mixing colors if the glasses are a neutral tint!

I use plenty of paper towels. I love paper towels! I use them for everything: to clean butcher's trays, to wipe brushes, to blot out and lighten sections of paintings, to stipple on paint, to wipe out washes, to wipe my hands, and sometimes my tears. To me, paper towels are a must.

Except for the matchbook covers that I use for squeegees, the only other good use I have for matches is to remove old stubborn paint caps. Light the match, rotate the cap of the tube in the flame for a few seconds, and remove the cap with a folded paper towel. If you burn your fingers, the cap remains stubborn, and you *need* this color, bite the tube in half!

REVIEW OF WATERCOLOR TECHNIQUES

To me, painting is a constant battle against monotony. To make my designs interesting, I try to include a variety of shapes, and I vary the sizes of the shapes I use. I also let warm and cool colors play against each other, pay careful attention to the arrangement of my lights and darks, and create excitement with many textural changes.

As you'll see throughout the demonstrations, I use the following techniques to achieve this variety. The first few are basic watercolor techniques; the rest can be used in almost any combination, at almost any stage of painting, to produce a wide range of exciting effects.

Flat Wash. *Take a 1" flat brush, load it with color, and apply it directly to either pre-wet or dry paper. Usually starting at the top, work down to the bottom of the area, using even amounts of color to create one value throughout.*

Graded Wash. *Use a large, 1" flat brush, load it with color, and paint onto either pre-wet or dry paper. Start your darkest strokes at the top, and gradually lighten them as you proceed downward. The transition should be gradual and smooth throughout.*

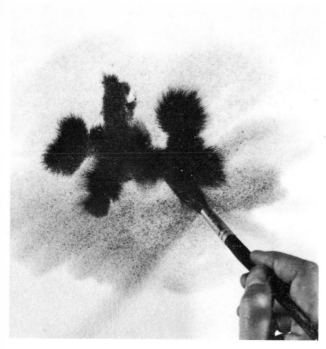

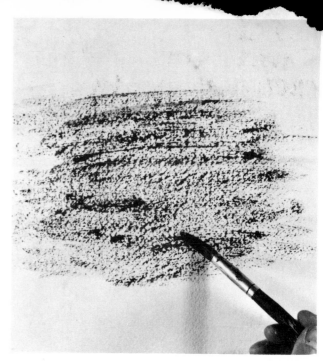

Wet-in-Wet. *After the first washes have been put down,* before *they're dry, load your brush and work back into them with thicker, deeper colors, which will spread and create soft edges.*

Drybrush. *Use either a flat or round brush and heavy color mixed with very little water. Drag your loaded brush across the* dry *paper, on its side, using rather quick strokes so the hairs deposit paint on the high spots of the paper and skip over the valleys, which will remain clean.*

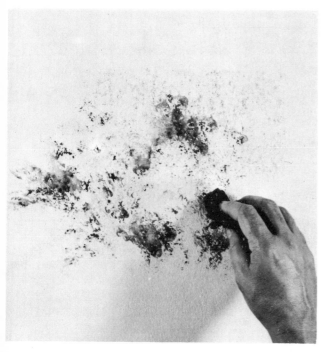

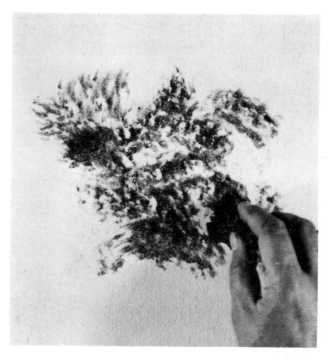

Sponging in Color Dry. *Moisten a natural sponge, dip it into undiluted color, and gently stipple it on dry paper to achieve the effect you want. By stippling, I mean that you should press the sponge onto the paper and lift it directly off; don't scrub. You can also create an interesting effect by pressing the loaded sponge on the paper and scrubbing, or moving it about 1/4" from the original point, before you lift it off the paper.*

Sponging in Color Wet. *Moisten a natural sponge, dip it into undiluted color, and gently stipple it on* damp *paper. Press and lift, with or without scrubbing, depending on the effect you want.*

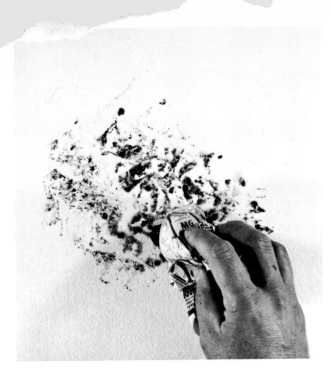

Applying Color with Crumpled Paper. *Use any paper. Crumple it up to the desired texture, pick up slightly diluted color from the palette, and stipple it either onto damp paper or directly onto dry paper.*

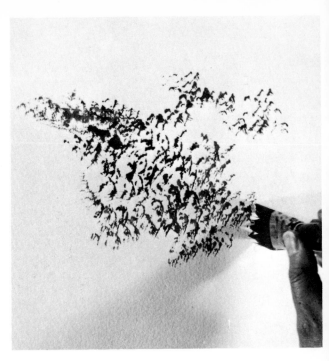

Dry Stipple. *Use a 1" flat brush. Pick up a mixture of paint on the brush and stipple it onto a* dry *surface. Notice the crisp, dry-edged effect of the stipple. Just touch the paper with the* tips *of the hairs and then lift. Don't scrub.*

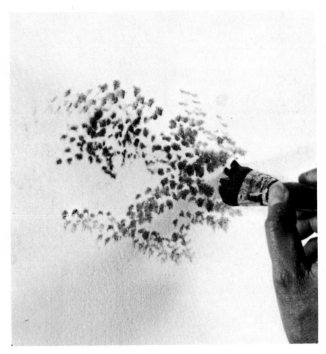

Wet Stipple. *Use a 1" flat brush. Dampen it, pick up a mixture of paint on the tip, and stipple onto* damp *paper for a diffuse effect.*

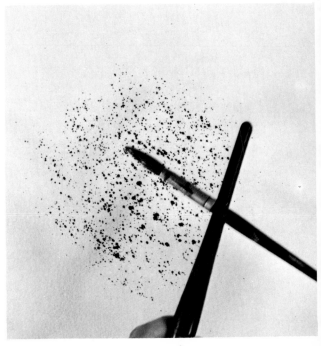

Dry Spatter. *Dip a No. 10 round brush into a deep mixture of diluted color, then gently tap it against the handle of another brush so that the paint spatters onto the* dry *paper.*

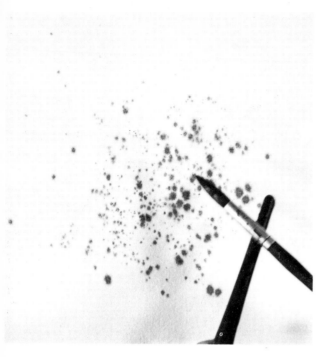

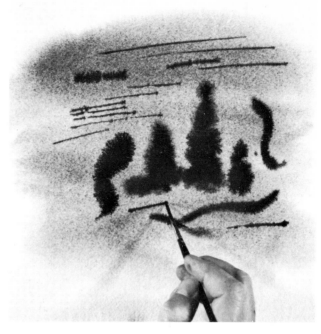

Wet Spatter. *Dip a No. 10 round brush into a deep mixture of diluted color, then gently tap it against the handle of another brush so that the paint spatters onto the* damp *paper.*

Applying Ink into Wet Color. *Use a medium-sized round brush. Dip the brush into pure ink and paint into a previously applied* damp *wash. You can also mix color with the ink. Enjoy the results!*

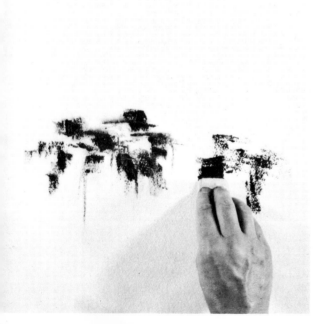

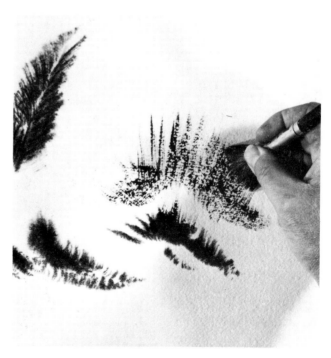

Applying Color with a Squeegee. *Fold a matchbook cover (or any heavy paper about the same size) in half, scoop up undiluted paint, and apply it in short strokes to either damp or dry paper.*

Fanning Out the Brush. *Hold a round or flat brush by the hairs, just where they emerge from the ferrule, and squeeze them into a fan between your thumb and first two fingers. Pick up a creamy mixture of paint, and apply it to either wet or dry paper, using short strokes.*

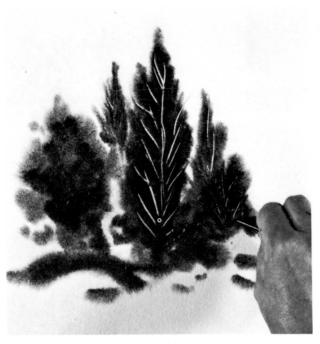

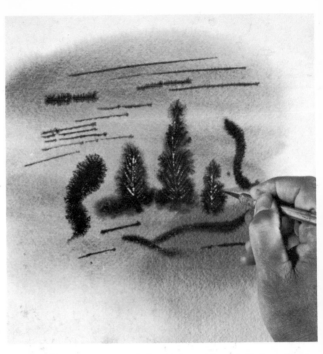

Squeezing Out with a Brush Handle. *When a large mass of dark pigment is half dry, use the back end of your brush to push a stroke down into the moist paint. This will squeeze the pigment out of the paper and leave a flashing light line.*

Scratching Out with a Blade. *Take a No. 11 X-Acto blade, or any sharp knife or instrument, and scratch out highlights on dry washes.*

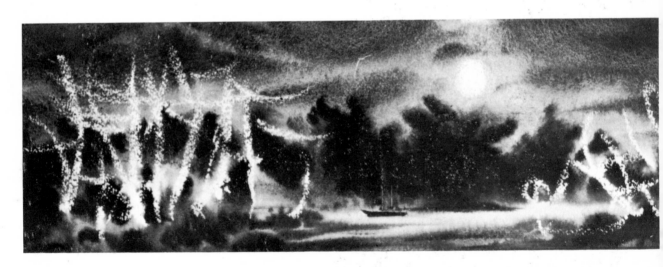

Covering with Wax. *(Above and Right) Draw your design in pencil and decide which areas you want to leave white. With a razor blade, cut a sharp edge on a block of paraffin and draw the edge of the wax over the areas that will remain white. As you apply your colors, the wax will repel them, and the white paper under the wax-covered areas will show through. This wax technique is especially effective for leaving delicate highlights in areas that you want to cover with broad washes of color.*

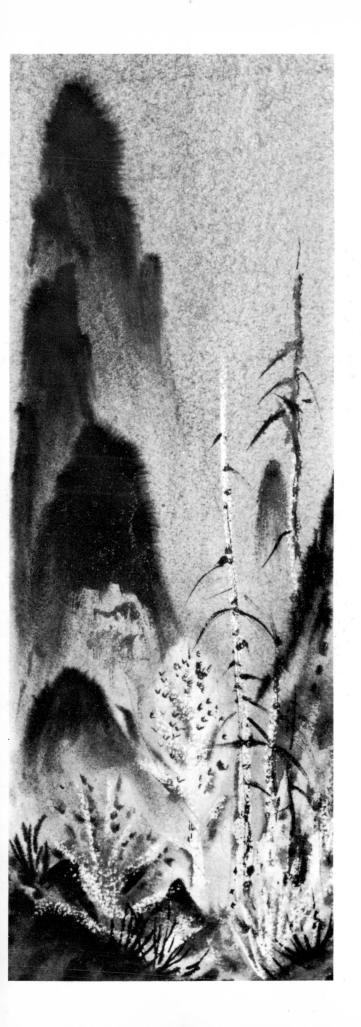

DEMONSTRATION 1

BRICK IN FLAT WASHES

The colors I'll use in this demonstration are cadmium red, burnt sienna, and cobalt blue. I'll use a half-sheet of Imperial size 300 lb. watercolor paper, but 140 lb. paper can also be used. I'll use a 1″ flat sabeline brush for my washes and a No. 6 round brush for texture; a No. 2 drawing pencil; a plastic eraser; a butcher's tray for my palette; paper towels; and a container of water. I've stretched the paper on plywood (a heavy drawing board will do as well) to make the paper lie flat and free of buckles.

Notice that, in this demonstration, I use three different values to establish form. To begin, I sketch a brick. Learn to use a heavy line as you sketch, so your drawings won't be lost in deep, dark washes as you paint over them. Remember also to squeeze out a generous amount of paint when you begin, so you won't run short as you progress.

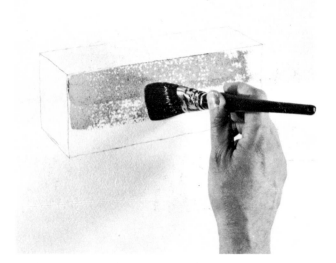

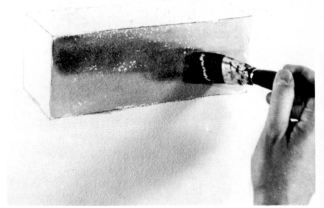

Step 1. *I brush a light wash of cadmium red and burnt sienna directly onto the paper. I call this a "dry" approach because I'm painting directly onto dry paper. With clean strokes, I work quickly and cover the entire front plane of the brick.*

Step 2. *Working rapidly, before the initial wash dries, I introduce an uneven pattern of cobalt blue into the wet wash. This mixture is not strong enough to overpower the other colors, but blends into them to create an uneven mixture of warm and cool colors, in a middle value range.*

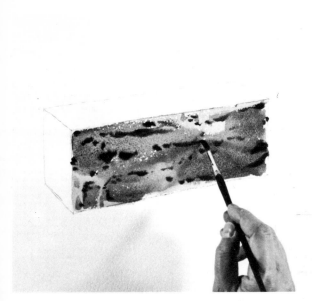

Step 3. *I prepare a thick mixture (almost straight tube color) of cobalt blue and burnt sienna, and stipple it into the wash while it's still damp with a No. 6 round brush. Then I mix black India ink into the thick mixture and stipple it into some areas to finish the texture on the front of the brick.*

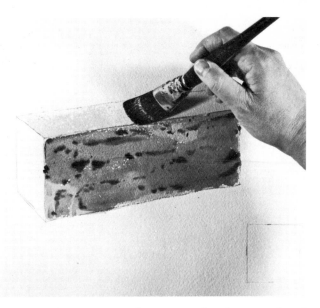

Step 4. *I paint a very pale mixture of cadmium red and burnt sienna onto the paper at the top of the brick. Then I introduce a small amount of cobalt blue unevenly into the wash, to create contrast between the warm and cool colors. As before, I stipple with a No. 6 brush and India ink for texture.*

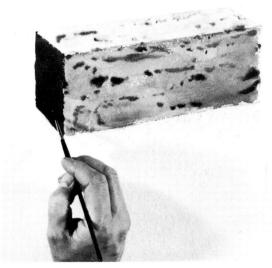

Step 5. *I paint a darker wash of burnt sienna, cobalt blue, and cadmium red into the left, shadow side of the brick. With the tip of the No. 6 brush, I stipple in a heavy mixture of cobalt blue, burnt sienna, and black India ink.*

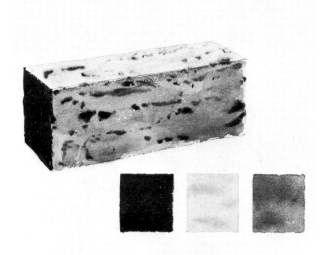

Step 6. *Here, I've broken down the three basic values so you can see them separately. I omitted the stippling to keep the values simple. As you can see, the dry approach is a fast, snappy way to create a quick impression of your subject.*

DEMONSTRATION 2

BRICK IN GRADED WASHES

I'll use the same colors that I used in the previous demonstration and a No. 10 round brush. My approach here will be to apply a graded wash to a pre-wet area of the paper. A graded wash is a wash of color, or colors, that gradually changes from a darker value to a lighter value as you work down, or across, the paper. Notice that, in this demonstration, the graded washes are all about the same value, and the form of the brick is determined by the way these washes are placed in relation to each other.

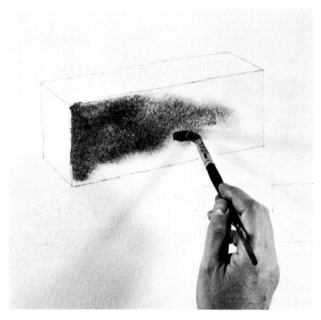

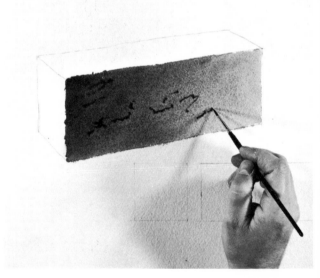

Step 1. *After sketching a brick with my No. 2 pencil, I wet the front part of the brick. I load my brush with burnt sienna and a touch of cadmium red and cobalt blue, and, starting in the upper left-hand corner, I gradually paint diagonally downward across the front of the brick, making my wash lighter and lighter in value as I approach the lower right-hand corner. I try to make this transition rather smooth.*

Step 2. *When the wash is complete and starting to dry, I add a little texture, using a No. 6 round sable brush loaded with black India ink, cobalt blue, and burnt sienna. I also add touches of black India ink by itself.*

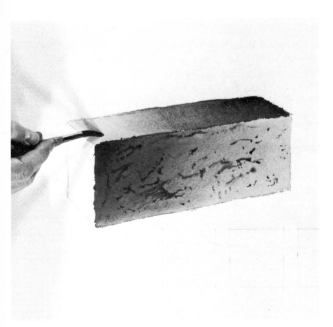

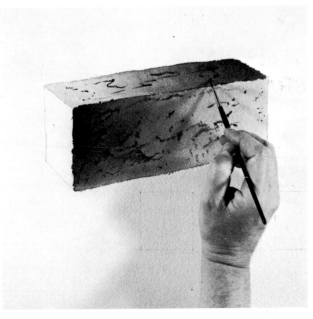

Step 3. *I use the same mixture that I used in Step 1 on the top of the brick; but here, I begin on the right side and make the wash lighter as I approach the left. Again, I make the gradation rather smooth, as though light were flowing across the surface.*

Step 4. *I use the small No. 6 round brush and the colors I used in Step 2 to add texture to the top surface of the brick. I make short, squiggly lines and use the tip of the brush to make points, making sure my large wash is still moist, so that the edges of these marks will soften slightly.*

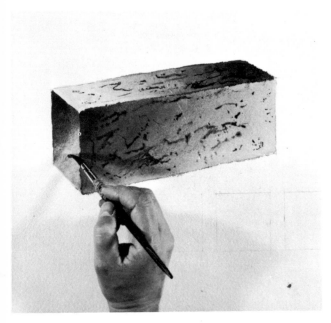

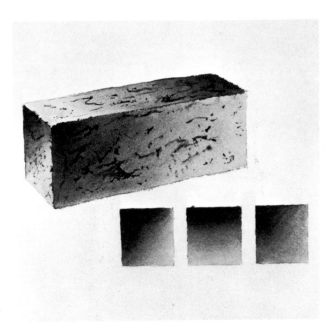

Step 5. *On the left side of the brick, I use the same mixture of burnt sienna and a touch of cadmium red and cobalt blue, this time running the graded wash down from the top left to the bottom right.*

Step. 6. *Once again, I stipple with the small brush, using ink, and the usual colors, varying the texture and bringing some texture over into the front and top areas to indicate small chips in the edges of the brick.*

DEMONSTRATION 3

CINDER BLOCK WET-IN-WET

The purpose of this demonstration is to introduce you to using the wet-in-wet technique to render a rather simple object. Although it's not very easy, you should master this technique, as you'll have many occasions to use it in your painting. I'll be using it extensively in the demonstrations throughout this book.

The colors I'll use here are cobalt blue, raw sienna, and burnt sienna, plus black India ink, applied with the brushes I used in the previous demonstrations.

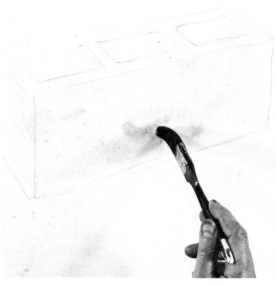

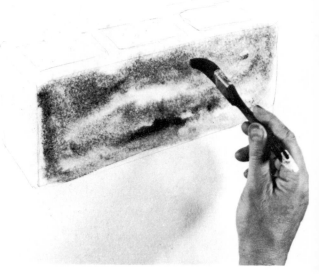

Step 1. *I wet the entire drawing—top, bottom, and sides—with clear water. I wet the surface twice, as water usually sinks into the paper the first time and dries too fast to allow the wet-in-wet approach. After I wet the paper the second time, I float a pale tint of raw sienna into the entire wet area.*

Step 2. *Into this pale wash, I introduce mixtures of cobalt blue and burnt sienna in broken and uneven amounts, to achieve a "vibration" of subtle color changes in the wash.*

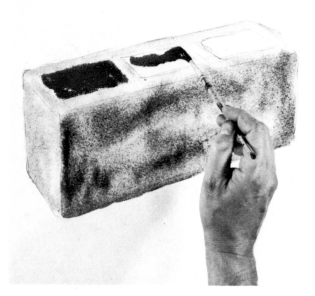

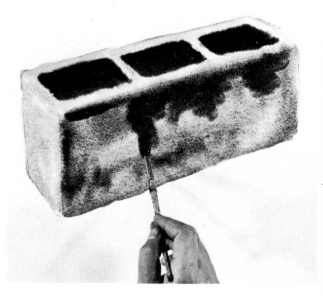

Step 3. *Now I paint the same color mixtures into the other areas with a small round brush and allow them to settle and start drying. I paint a thick mixture of cobalt blue and burnt sienna into the area where I've penciled in the holes in the top of the block.*

Step 4. *I paint some of the same mixture of burnt sienna and cobalt blue into the wet front part of the block and drag it down with the smaller round brush to create a broken, graded wash effect. I use this deeper value to create a feeling of form.*

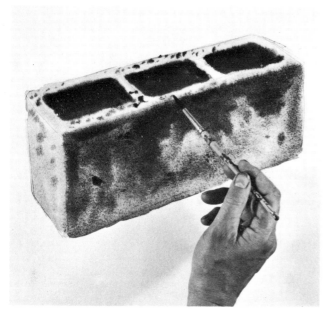

Step 5. *Again, with the small No. 6 round brush loaded with ink and thick mixtures of cobalt blue and burnt sienna, I stipple in the texture of cinder. I try to vary the feeling of this stipple effect as I use it.*

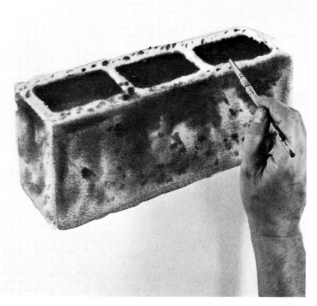

Step 6. *I add pure India ink to the areas in the far ends of the holes to strengthen the feeling of their depth, blending the ink gently with the wet color.*

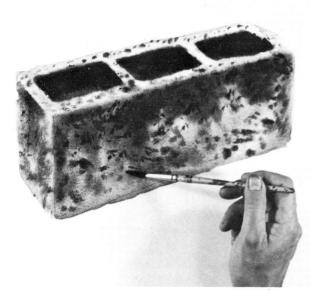

Step 7. *I add more texture using a mixture of cobalt blue and burnt sienna applied with the side of the small brush to vary the effects.*

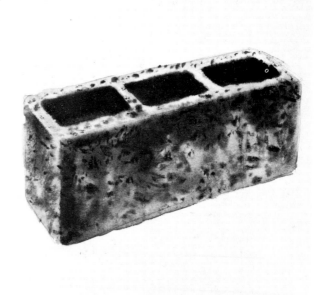

Step 8. *On the completed cinder block, I strengthen the value at the lower left front corner to help distinguish the three different planes of the block. With pure black India ink, I also add some small textural effects here and there to complete the cinder effect.*

DEMONSTRATION 4

CHIMNEY AND ROOFTOP WET-IN-WET

Now, let's put some of the techniques I've shown you to work on different subject matter. Instead of a cinder block, I'll paint a whole chimney. I'll also paint a shingled roof and part of a house, but don't let this throw you. Although the subjects are different, the techniques are the same. Here, I'll use a No. 10 round brush, a No. 6 round brush, and a No. 2 round brush. My colors will be cadmium red, raw sienna, cobalt blue, burnt sienna, and black India ink.

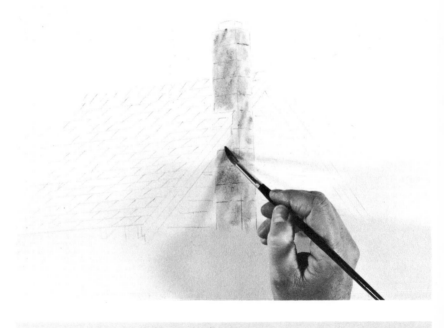

Step 1. *I wet the chimney area with clear water and add a light wash of raw sienna. Then I flood in uneven mixtures of burnt sienna and cobalt blue in broken, wet patches, letting the different colors work and "vibrate" nicely together.*

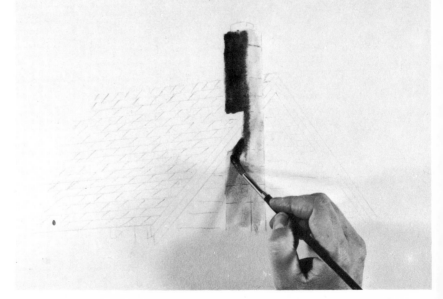

Step 2. *I mix a thick, rich mixture of cobalt blue and burnt sienna and paint it into the existing wet wash to indicate the shadow side of the chimney. (Always pace the drying of the first wash. If it's too wet when you add the shadow pigments, they'll spread too much.)*

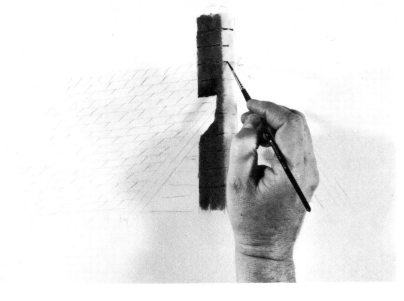

Step 3. *Here, I use a No. 2 round brush and India ink to draw in the mortar joints. (When you use ink, test to be sure you don't have too much on the brush, or it will run out and spread too much. Dip your brush into the ink and palette it out by moving it back and forth across a piece of scrap paper until you have the right amount of ink left in the brush.)*

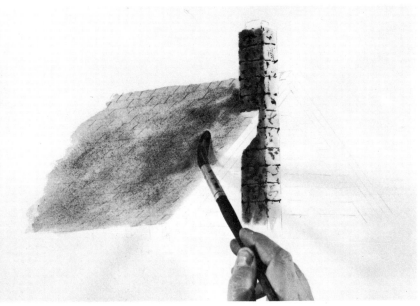

Step 4. *With stipples of black ink, cobalt blue, and burnt sienna, I complete the textural effect of cinder block. Now, I wet the roof area with clear water and introduce a varied wash of raw sienna, burnt sienna, cobalt blue, and cadmium red.*

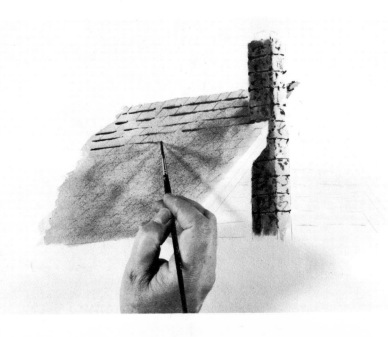

Step 5. *When these washes begin to settle into the paper, I draw into them the shingle pattern with a No. 6 round brush and pure black India ink. I work quite rapidly, to complete the pattern before the wash dries completely.*

Step 6. *Notice that I add some extra shadows and stains to the roof to break up the overall monotony. With a No. 2 brush, I paint a mixture of raw sienna and cobalt blue on dry paper for the fascia boards, strengthening it with slight touches of ink. Then I do the same for the roof shingles on the far right side of the roof. With a No. 6 round brush, I paint some raw sienna under the roof overhang. I mix a little cobalt blue into the raw sienna, but I keep the mixture on the warm, yellowish side.*

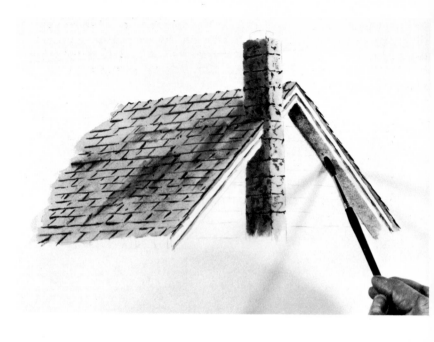

Step 7. *For the clapboard shingles, I paint a direct wash of very pale cadmium red; then I quickly add very pale tints of cobalt blue unevenly throughout the wash. I suggest the shingles with the smaller brush and pure black ink.*

Step 8. *With my little finger, I deliberately smudge just a couple of the India ink lines on the shingles while they're still damp, to break up the monotony of line. I paint the tile chimney flue in tints of pure cadmium red and raw sienna, mixed to a near-orange color.*

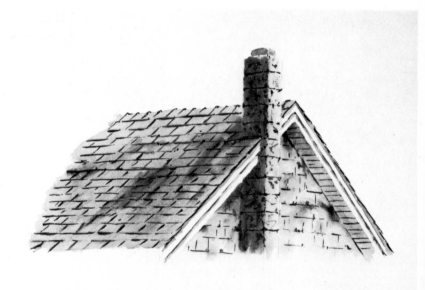

In this demonstration, I'll use the dry approach, and I'll show you how to use drybrush with both paint and ink. For this demonstration, I'll use a stretched sheet of 300 lb. rough paper (15″ x 22″), a large flat 1″ brush, a No. 10, and a No. 6 round brush. My colors will be burnt sienna, raw sienna, cobalt blue, and India ink.

DEMONSTRATION 5

OLD BOARDS IN DRYBRUSH

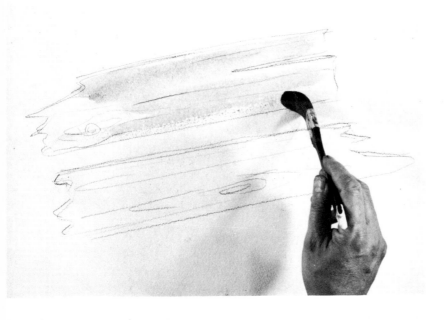

Step 1. *With the 1″ flat brush, I paint a pale tint of raw sienna directly onto the dry paper.*

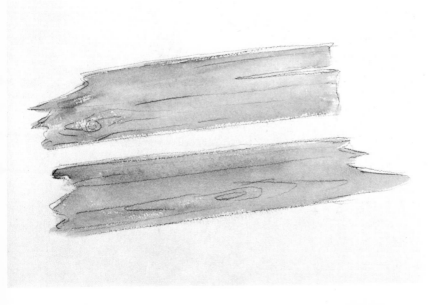

Step 2. *Into this, I add touches of burnt sienna and cobalt blue, mixed to a cool gray. I wash this on unevenly over the board and let it dry.*

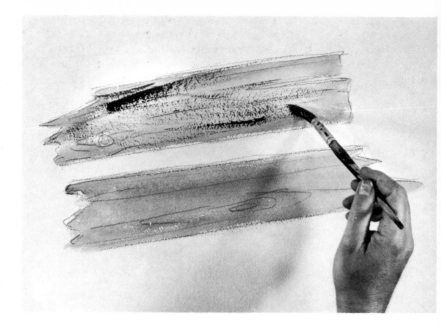

Step 3. *With a No. 10 round brush, I drybrush cobalt blue and burnt sienna over the dry wash, keeping the paint a little on the thick side.*

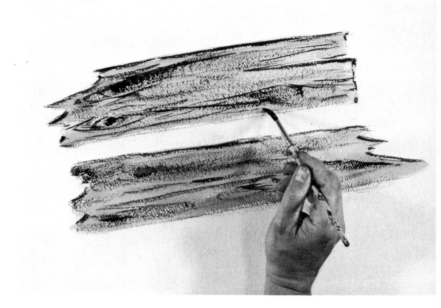

Step 4. *I add more drybrush for texture, using the same colors and black ink. Using a smaller brush, I draw in some lines to depict knot-holes and the grain of the wood.*

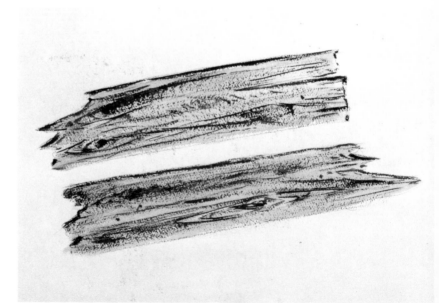

Step 5. *To complete the effect, I add a bit more texture with drybrush and ink.*

Now I'll show you how to create the varied textures of old wood with the wet-in-wet technique. These textures will be somewhat softer than the textures created by drybrush, and the overall effect will be somewhat more unified. The colors I'll use are cadmium red, cobalt blue, burnt sienna, and black India ink; I'll use the usual brushes.

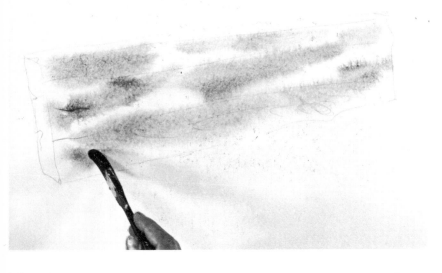

Step 1. *First, I wet the entire sketch of the board with clear water. Then I flood pale tints of cadmium red into this wet area with a large, flat brush.*

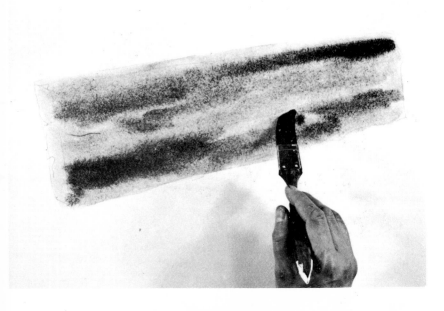

Step 2. *Now, I mix cobalt blue and burnt sienna and add this mixture to the wet wash in uneven amounts, letting it spread and settle into the paper.*

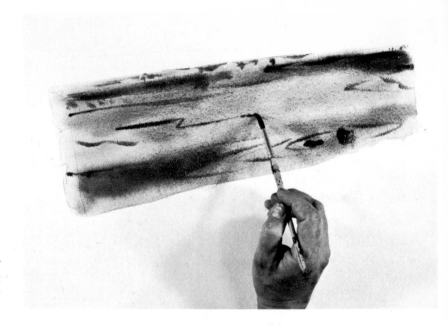

Step 3. *With a small, round brush, I work a thick mixture of burnt sienna and cobalt blue into this semi-dry wash to indicate some grain texture.*

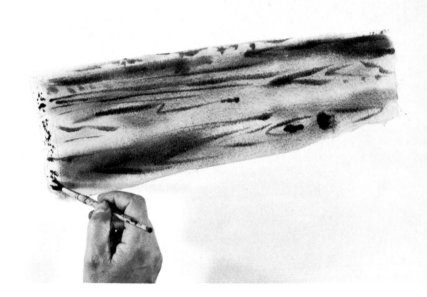

Step 4. *To depict the end grain of the wood, I stipple a thick mixture of ink, cobalt blue, and burnt sienna into the end of the board.*

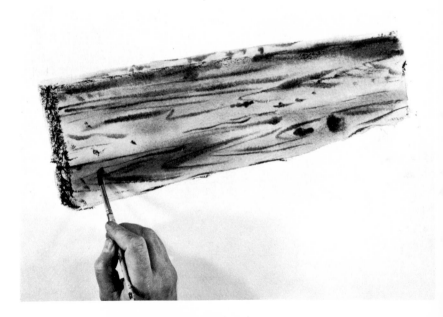

Step 5. *With thick mixtures of the same colors and pure India ink, I add more grain texture to give the picture a feeling of reality and a better design structure.*

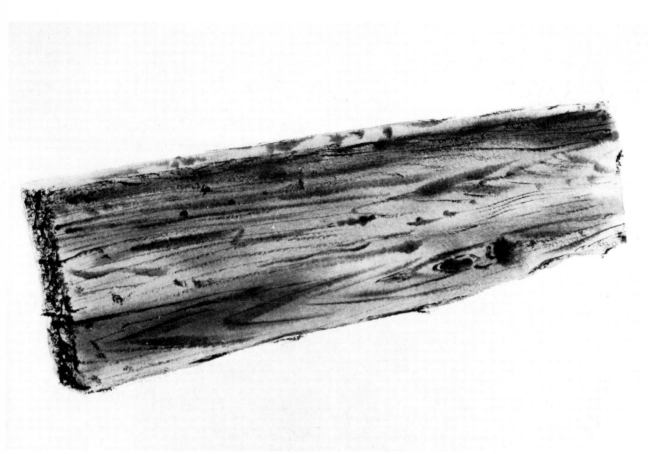

Step 6. *To the washes, I add more fine lines with drybrush. The washes of the main body of color are not quite dry, so the drybrush has a soft effect. Notice the difference in texture between this wet-in-wet demonstration and the drybrush texture created in Demonstration 5.*

DEMONSTRATION 7

WOODEN SHED WET-IN-WET

In this demonstration, I'll use the wet-in-wet technique again. This time, instead of wetting the entire building area with clear water, I'll work on it in sections. My palette contains cadmium red, cobalt blue, burnt sienna, and black India ink. To begin, I've stretched a half-sheet of cold-pressed Imperial-size (15″ x 22″) watercolor paper on a plywood board.

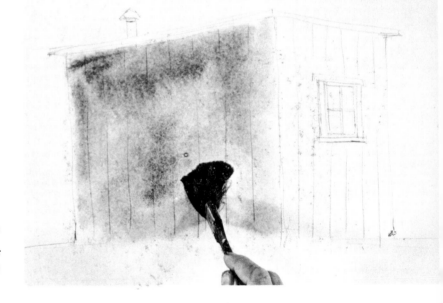

Step 1. *I wet just the left wall of the shed with clear water. Using a 1″ flat brush, I spread a very pale tint of cadmium red, burnt sienna, and cobalt blue into this wet wash.*

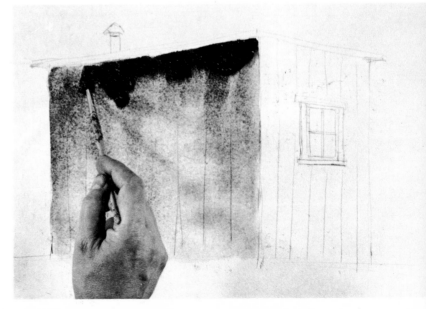

Step 2. *I dip a small No. 6 round brush into the ink and feed it into the top of the wet wash to establish the dark area under the edge of the roof, where light is not reflected very well.*

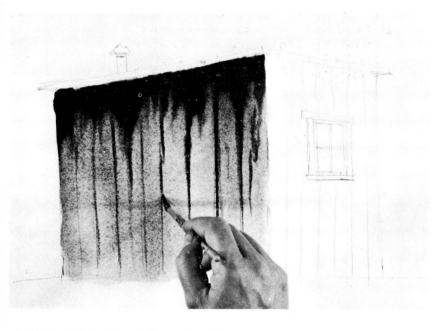

Step 3. *With a small No. 2 brush, I drag the ink down into the semi-wet wash to indicate the boards of the shack.*

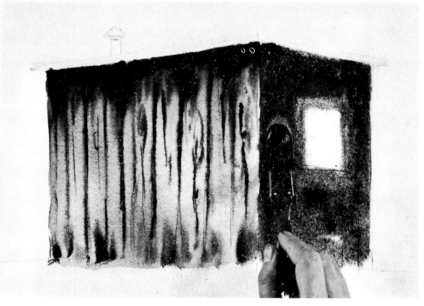

Step 4. *Now I strengthen some tones at the bottom left of the shack with deeper mixtures of the colors I used in Step 1, and add more texture to the boards with ink. I wet the right side of the shack with clear water and float a darker wash of cobalt blue, burnt sienna, and cadmium red into this wet area, leaving white paper where I've sketched in the window.*

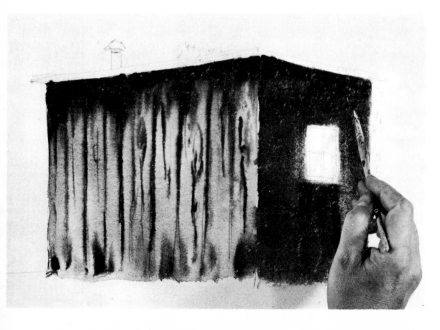

Step 5. *I strengthen the area under the roof with pure India ink, dropping it into the existing wet wash with a No. 6 round brush.*

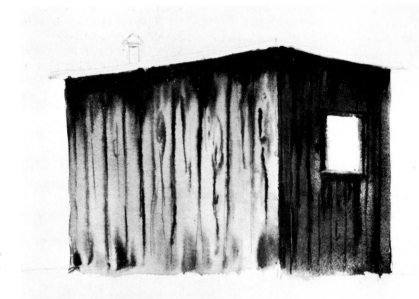

Step 6. *Adding ink to the brush as I need it, I drag a small No. 2 round brush downward to indicate board lines on the right wall. Again, I leave the window area white.*

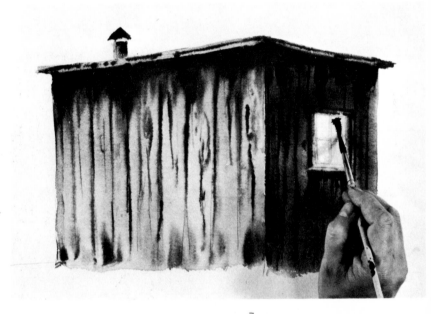

Step 7. *Now I paint each windowpane with a mixture of burnt sienna and cobalt blue. While this wash is still wet, I add India ink in small areas to give depth to each windowpane. Allowing the window area to dry, I paint in the edge of the roof and the vent stack. I wet each of these areas first with clear water. Then I fill them in with a mixture of color and ink, using the same light and dark washes I used on the left side of the shack, in the same order.*

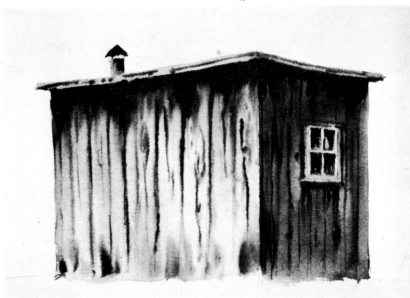

Step 8. *After the panes dry, I finish the window trim with a gray mixture of cobalt blue and burnt sienna.*

In this demonstration, I'll show you how to use the wet-in-wet technique in painting trees—to create the soft effect of pines against the sky. I'll also show you how to use a sponge to add color and texture.

As usual, I've soaked a half-sheet of 300 lb. watercolor paper and stretched it on a plywood board. I'll use a No. 6 and a No. 10 round brush, and a 1″ flat brush, to render the sky and trees. My colors will be burnt sienna, sap green, and cobalt blue. To begin, I've made a dark, rough pencil sketch of two pine trees.

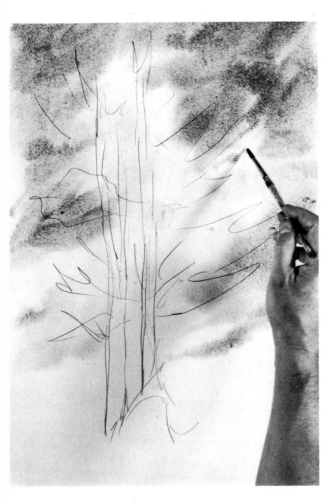

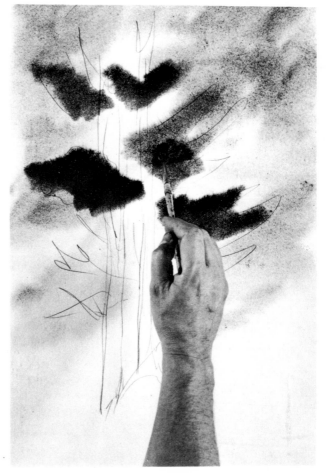

Step 1. *I wet the entire sheet with clear water. (A double wetting is necessary here, to keep the paper wet a long time.) I flood the wet area with a slightly warm gray mixture of cobalt blue and burnt sienna, using a 1″ flat brush, to indicate clouds. Then I introduce some spots of blue between the clouds with a No. 6 round brush.*

Step 2. *I paint thick mixtures of sap green and cobalt blue into the wet sky, as the first step in rendering the pine foliage.*

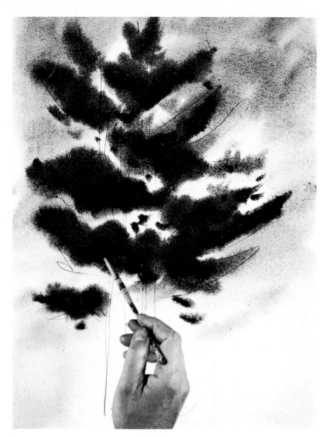

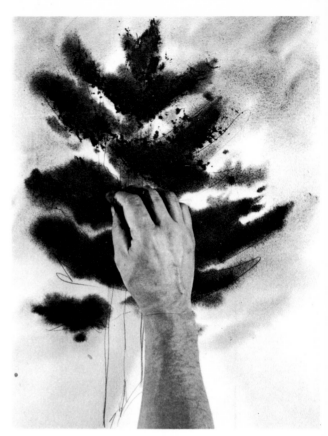

Step 3. *I introduce a mixture of cobalt blue and burnt sienna into this foliage area. Then, to warm up the colors and make them vibrate, I add a mixture of cobalt blue and burnt sienna, leaning toward burnt sienna, here and there in light touches.*

Step 4. *I take a sponge, moisten it with clear water, squeeze it out, and dip it into India ink that I've poured out onto a corner of my large palette. I dip the sponge into pure cobalt blue, burnt sienna, and sap green to load it with each color, and stipple it into the pine clusters.*

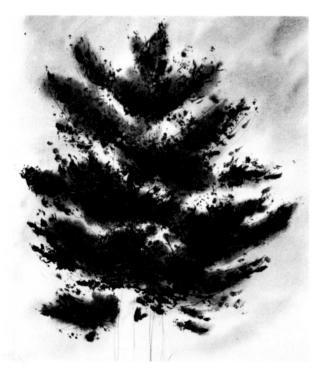

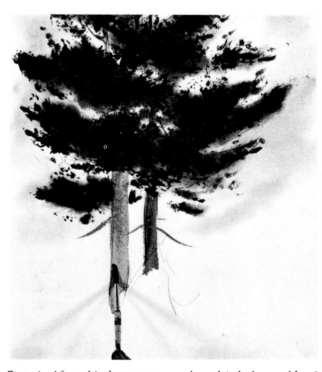

Step 5. *You can see how this sponge stippling deepens the value and adds texture to the foliage. I always make sure that the paper is not too wet when I stipple ink and color into it, so it won't blend too much. Here again, you'll have to learn by trial and error.*

Step 6. *After this last maneuver has dried thoroughly, I take the No. 6 brush and paint a warm wash of burnt sienna for the tree trunks.*

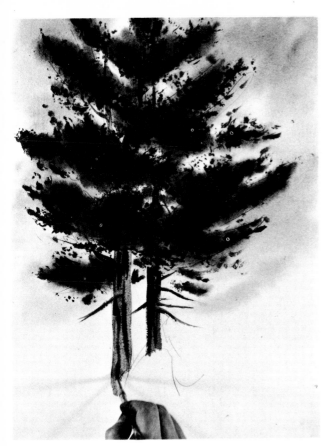 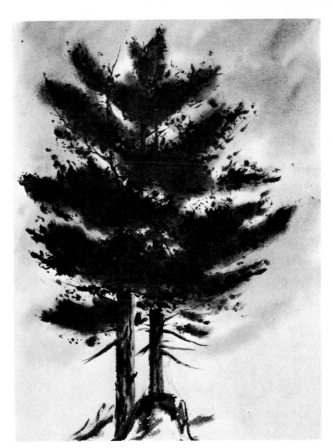

Step 7. *I dip the small brush into India ink and add texture to the trunks. Pure ink can be used to create different gray values as it mixes with a burnt sienna wash and becomes diluted.*

Step 8. *Here, I complete the trees by adding the feeling of rocks and earth to the base area of the trunks. Notice the way the textures in the tree trunks and foliage complement each other.*

DEMONSTRATION 9

FOREGROUND WET-IN-WET AND DRYBRUSH

Here, I'll demonstrate a method that will give you a little more control of your washes and help you create a crisper feeling than you can using wet-in-wet alone. You can make your subject appear much sharper when you use this treatment. The tools I'll use are a sponge, a No. 6 round brush, and a 1″ flat brush. My colors will be raw sienna, cobalt blue, burnt sienna, sap green, and black India ink. I'll begin by making a rough sketch of some shrubs, bushes, grass, and rocks, on a 300 lb. sheet of paper.

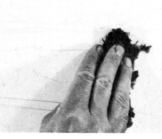

Step 1. *I use a clean sponge to soak the entire foreground area with clear water. I double-wet this area to insure against its drying too soon.*

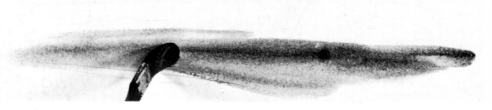

Step 2. *I load a 1″ flat brush with a mixture of cobalt blue and burnt sienna and "swipe" it into the wet paper. I try to keep the paint mixtures ranging back and forth from warm to cool: cooler in the background and warmer in the foreground.*

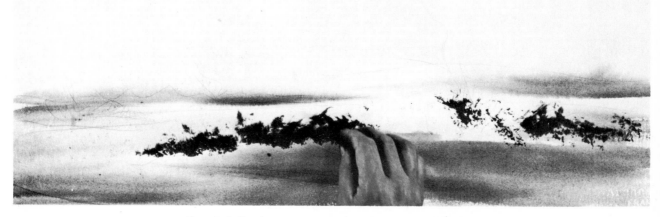

Step 3. *I dip the sponge into the ink, then into cobalt blue and sap green, and stipple in texture for the small shrubs, bushes, and grass. Then I add some burnt sienna to the mixture on the sponge to strengthen the texture and design.*

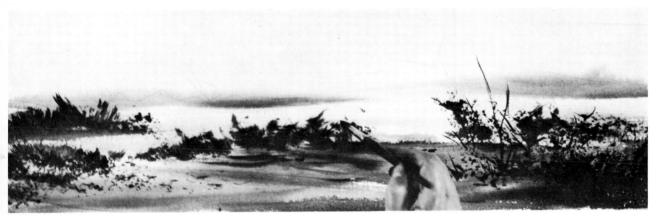

Step 4. *Using the small round No. 6 brush, I add suggestions of twigs and branches on the half-bare bushes. I also throw some small stipple marks into the foreground with the tip of the brush for texture and decorative accent.*

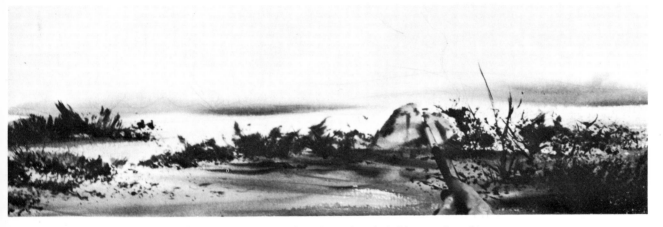

Step 5. *When the ground washes are dry, I paint the rock with a pale cobalt blue wash and accent it with a mixture of cobalt blue and burnt sienna, keeping this mixture thick and on the warm, burnt sienna side.*

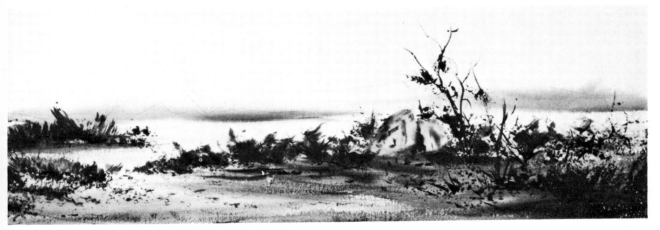

Step 6. *I use a thick mixture of burnt sienna and cobalt blue for some drybrush over the foreground. I also use this drybrush mixture to suggest some dried leaves.*

FOREGROUND WET-IN-WET

The following approach is best to use when you want a strong-valued foreground that is *not* the focal point of the picture; when you want to look *over*, or *past*, the foreground to a *different* center of interest. I'll use the same brushes and colors as before, and a stretched sheet of 300 lb. cold-pressed paper.

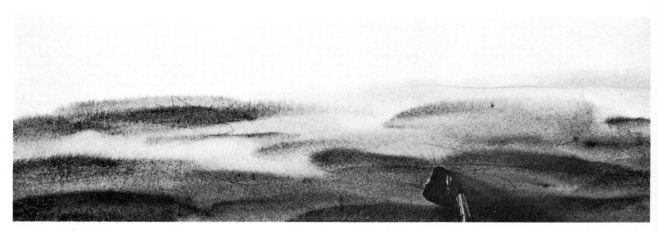

Step 1. *After I double-wet the foreground area with clear water, I take my 1" flat brush and mix warm and cool values of cobalt blue and burnt sienna directly on the wet paper, letting them bleed unevenly onto the paper.*

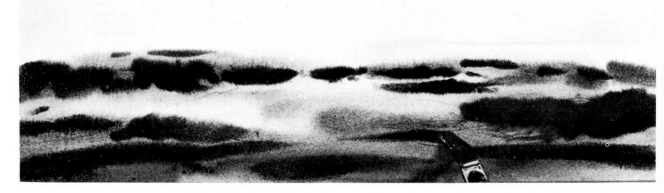

Step 2. *As the washes begin to settle into the paper, I strengthen the design with stronger and thicker mixtures of cobalt blue, burnt sienna, and sap green to suggest grass and shrubs.*

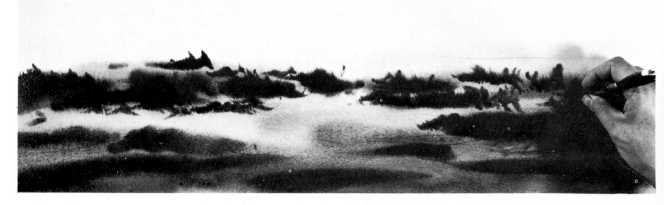

Step 3. *Using the same mixtures of cobalt blue, burnt sienna, and sap green, I squeeze the hairs of the brush, where they emerge from the ferrule, making a fan effect. Holding the brush this way, I load it with color and paint short, upward strokes to suggest tufts of grass.*

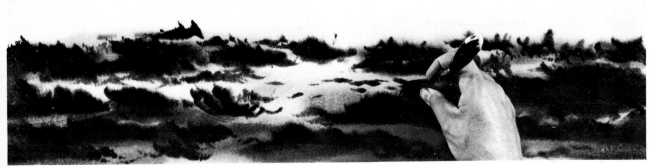

Step 4. *Using the same fanned-out brush approach, I add India ink to the mixture and continue to render the shrubs and suggest the small formations in the foreground.*

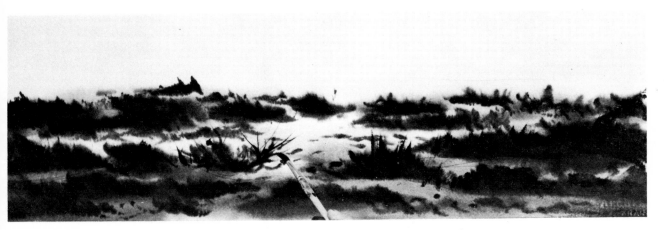

Step 5. *With my small No. 6 round brush, loaded with black ink and burnt sienna, I stroke in suggestions of twigs, branches, and tufts of grass.*

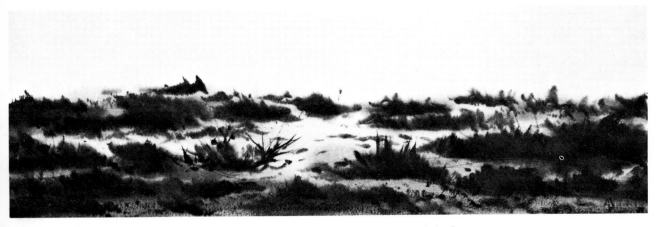

Step 6. *When this is dry, I add a hint of texture with drybrush to the front of the foreground, for a change of pace.*

DEMONSTRATION 11

SKY WET-IN-WET, DIRECT APPROACH

In this demonstration, I'll show you how to paint a typical wet-in-wet sky. This will be a heavy, overcast sky, with the sun just starting to break through. The 1″ flat brush is all I'll use. My colors will be cadmium red, burnt sienna, cobalt blue, and permanent blue.

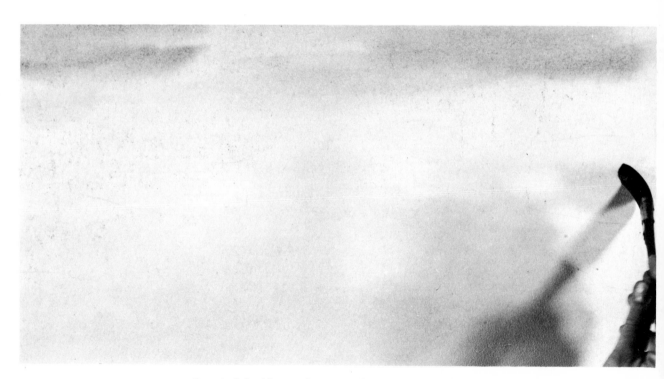

Step 1. *I double-wet the paper thoroughly, applying clear water with a clean sponge. I mix a pale tint of burnt sienna and cadmium red and spread it evenly throughout the bottom half of the sky area—not in the middle, which should remain white. I also add some of this pale tint in separate strokes to the top section and corners of the sky.*

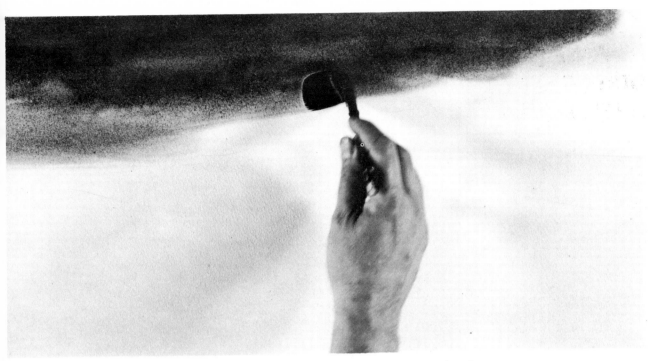

Step 2. *I add cobalt blue and a touch of permanent blue to burnt sienna in warm and cool mixtures, right on the wet paper. I try to control the values, and, since I'm applying the color directly to the wet wash on the paper, this calls for speed. I try not to go back into the large wash areas too often. Instead, I make the necessary value adjustments quickly in the beginning and then let them settle into the paper.*

Step 3. *Here, you can see the final results. The high cloud at the top of the picture is larger, darker, and somewhat warmer than the others. The rest of the clouds are thinner, and they seem to recede and drift as they become lighter and cooler toward the middle, where the light is breaking through.*

DEMONSTRATION 12

SKY WET-IN-WET, UNDERPAINTING

Now, I'll show you a good way to control your washes as you paint a backlit sky (clouds lit by the sun from *behind*). The 1" flat brush is all I'll need. My colors will be the same as in the last demonstration.

Step 1. *I double-wet the paper thoroughly with a sponge and clear water. I mix a tint of cadmium red and burnt sienna and apply it to the sides of the sky area, bleeding it in lighter toward the middle, where I leave a section of paper white. Now I mix burnt sienna and cobalt blue into this wash to strengthen and deepen the values.*

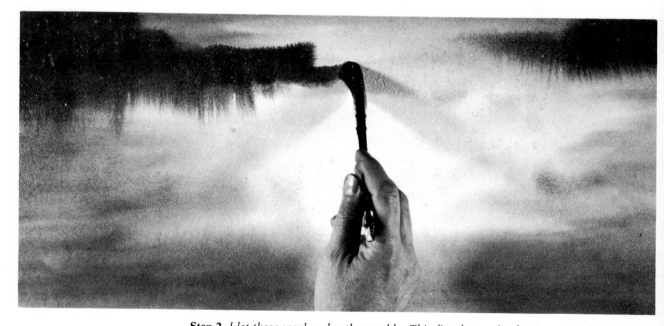

Step 2. *I let these washes dry thoroughly. This first layer of value is an "underpainting." I want to make the center of the sky the brightest area, so I re-wet this area by literally pouring a jar of water over it. (When I do this, I usually take the painting outside into the garden, pour the jar of water over the area I want to wet, and let most of it run off. As long as my underwashes aren't exceptionally deep, this technique doesn't disturb them noticeably.) Then I tilt the board, let most of the water run off, and let the rest of the water settle until I have the degree of wetness I want.*

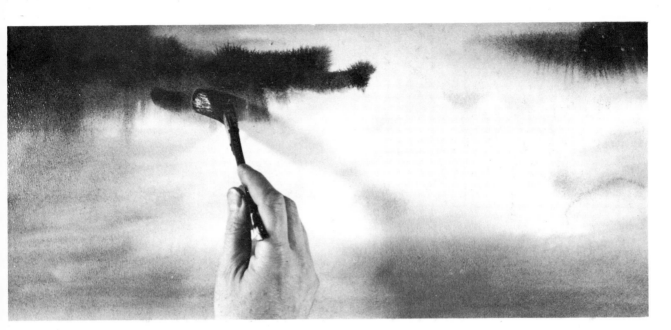

Step 3. *I continue to adjust the warm and cool values of the sky by applying and mixing the same colors right on the wet paper, keeping in mind the drying time and working quickly.*

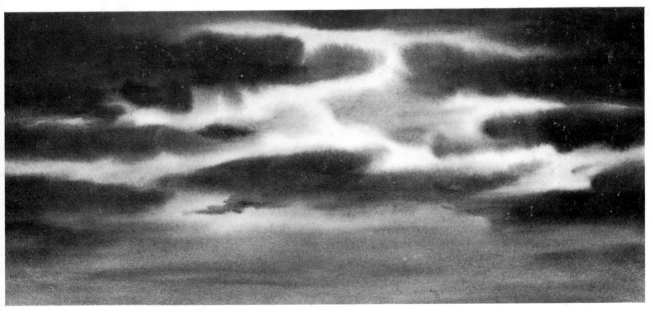

Step 4. *See that the finished sky has the backlit effect I'm after: the clouds are in perspective, appearing thinner as they recede into the background, and the sun seems to show through from behind.*

DEMONSTRATION 13

OLD SHED
IN FOREST
SURROUNDINGS

Here, I'm going to bring together the techniques I've been showing you
to produce a finished picture of a shed, sky, and trees. I'll work most of
this picture wet-in-wet, in sections. My palette will contain cobalt blue,
burnt sienna, cadmium red, sap green, raw sienna, and black India ink.
My brushes will be 1″ flat, No. 6 round and No. 2 round; I'll also use
sponges.

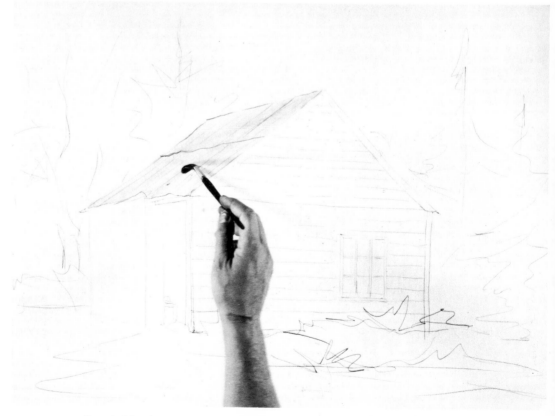

Step 1. *I load a wet No. 6 round brush with a pale tint of cadmium red and wash in the
metal roof.*

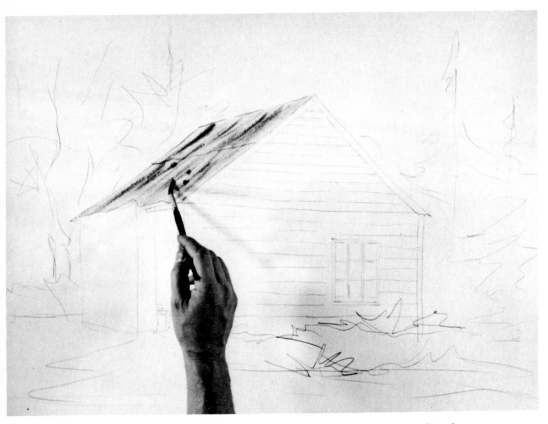

Step 2. *With the same brush, I unevenly brush in some pure burnt sienna, making long strokes that run parallel to the edge of the roof.*

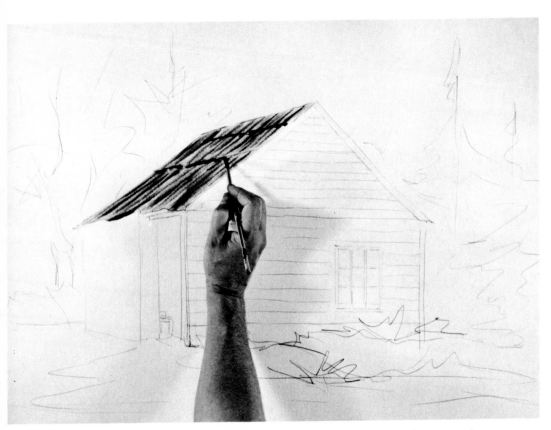

Step 3. *With a mixture of black India ink and burnt sienna, I add the texture of corrugated metal. Then I add an accent here and there with pure India ink.*

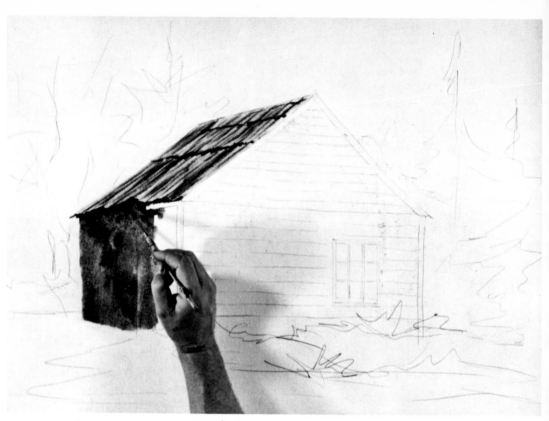

Step 4. *I wet the concrete sidewall of the shed with clear water, and, with a No. 6 brush, I float in uneven mixtures of raw sienna and cobalt blue. I add a dark shadow of pure India ink under the metal roof.*

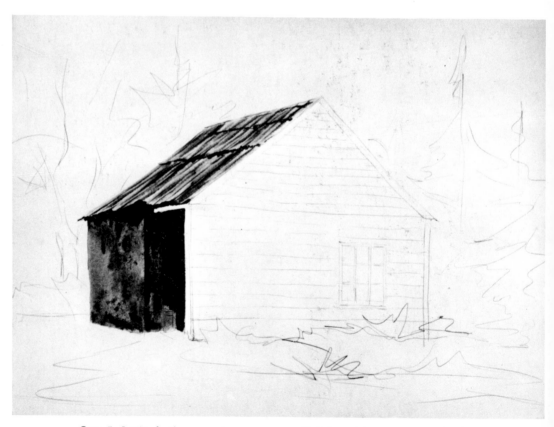

Step 5. *I stipple the concrete area ever so lightly, with a sponge and ink. Using a dark, heavy mixture of cobalt blue and burnt sienna, I render the dark, open doorway with a No. 6 brush. I leave an area of lighter wash to indicate the old box in the bottom left corner of the doorway.*

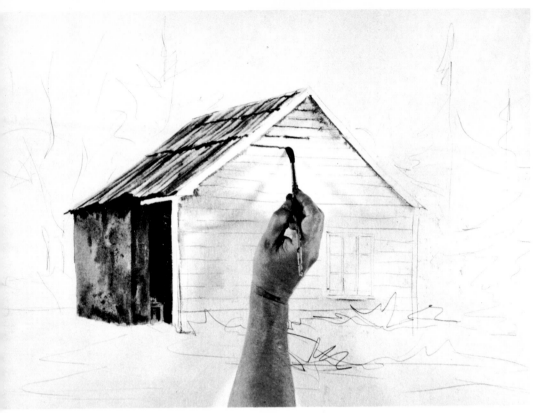

Step 6. *I wet the entire front of the shed with clear water. Then, using a 1" flat brush, I drop in very pale, uneven tints of cadmium red and cobalt blue. To indicate the wood siding, I load my No. 6 brush with pure ink, palette it out until it forms a chisel-like point, and render the wood siding.*

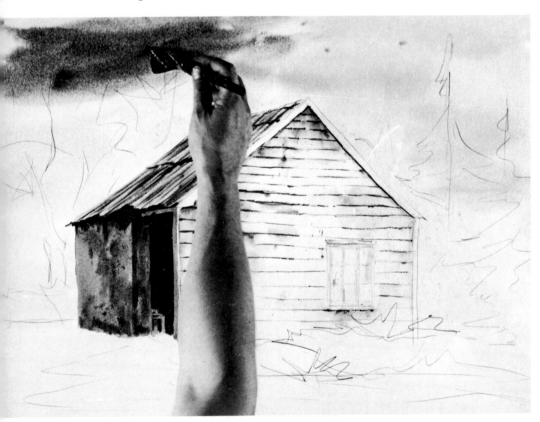

Step 7. *Now I wet the entire sky area with a sponge and clear water. I float in the sky by mixing cobalt blue and burnt sienna directly on the paper with a 1" flat brush. I keep these paint mixtures on the cooler side for the sky. I add a touch of drybrush texture and smudge it with my little finger to indicate texture and stains on the wood siding.*

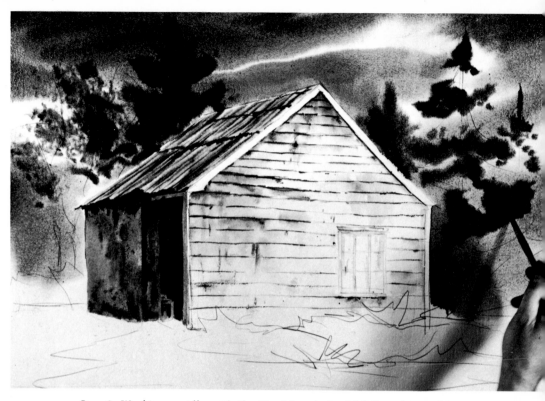

Step 8. *Working rapidly with the No. 6 brush, I add foliage by working sap green, raw sienna, cobalt blue, and touches of burnt sienna into the wet sky. Then I stipple the area lightly with dark mixtures of the same colors on a sponge.*

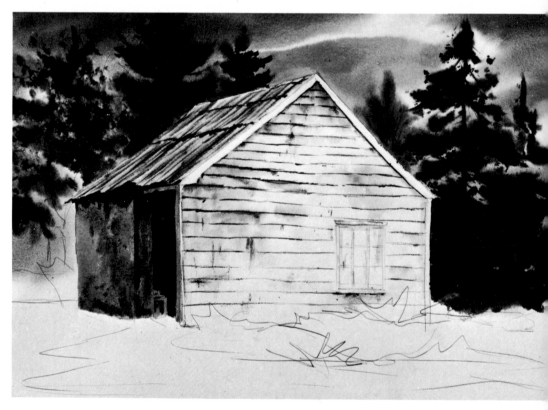

Step 9. *I load the same brush with ink and heavy mixtures of cobalt blue, sap green, and burnt sienna, and indicate the darkest foliage areas. Then I stipple the area with a sponge loaded with the same mixtures of paint and ink.*

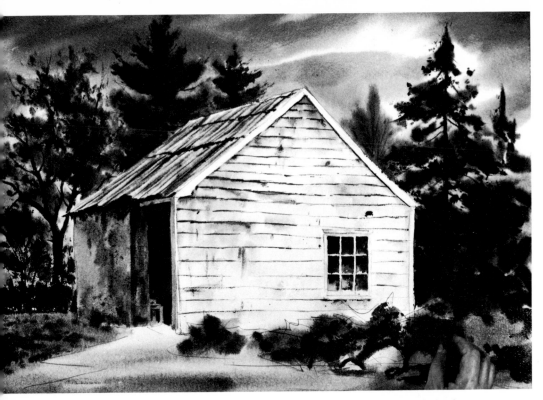

Step 10. *Using the dark, greenish mixtures I have on my palette, I paint the area of shrubs on the left, toward the rear of the shed. I paint the window, using cadmium red and cobalt blue, plus ink. With burnt sienna and black ink, I paint in the tree trunks and branches to the left behind the shed. I wet the foreground area and paint in burnt sienna, cobalt blue, and raw sienna in uneven washes. While these are still wet, I sponge in sap green, burnt sienna, and cobalt blue to indicate shrubs and low bushes.*

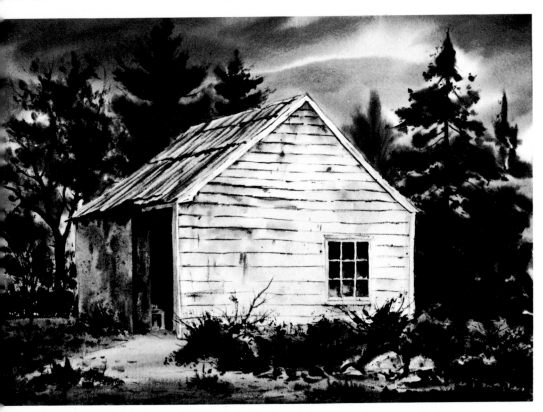

Step 11. *I add ink to the green mixtures on my palette, load my sponge, and stipple the foreground. I use a No. 2 brush loaded with ink and burnt sienna to suggest branches in the foreground. I render the rocks in the right foreground with a pale wash of cobalt blue. Then I accentuate the rocks with a mixture of cobalt blue and burnt sienna.*

In this demonstration, I'll show you how to deal with the problems of painting subjects in bright sunlight. My subject this time is a white stucco house, in front lighting, in early morning.

I'll use cobalt blue, burnt sienna, sap green, raw sienna, cadmium red, and black India ink. My brushes will include a No. 2, No. 6, and No. 10 round, and a 1″ flat brush. I'll use natural sponges, cold-pressed, Arches pre-mounted watercolor board; and, for this demonstration, I'll use some pieces of light cardboard.

STUCCO HOUSE IN BRIGHT SUNLIGHT

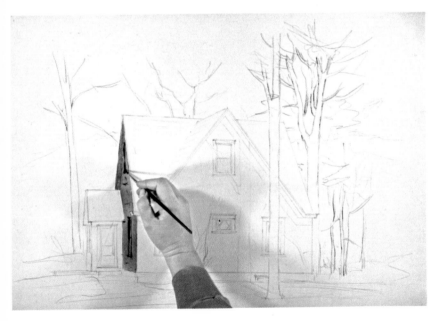

Step 1. *With a bluish mixture of cobalt blue and cadmium red, I wash in the shadow side of the house. Then I gently stroke in some raw sienna to warm this section up with indications of reflected light. While this wash is still damp, I paint in suggestions of windows with burnt sienna and black ink.*

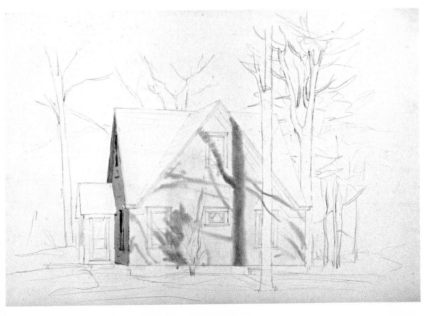

Step 2. *I wet the front wall of the house with clear water and warm up this white area in a few places with pale touches of raw sienna. With a No. 6 round brush, I add dark tree shadows in cobalt blue and burnt sienna and warm up the shadows here and there with raw sienna.*

Step 3. *I add the cast shadow across the small doorway with a mixture of cadmium red, cobalt blue, and raw sienna. I use cobalt blue and a touch of cadmium red to indicate the cast shadow on the wall by the roof, and I warm up the shadow on the underside of the roof with a bit of raw sienna.*

Step 4. *I double-wet the entire area around the building, from the bottom of the house up, with clear water. I wash in the sky with a 1" flat brush loaded with cobalt blue and touches of burnt sienna and sap green. Then, to indicate the mountain behind the house, I introduce deep purple mixtures of cobalt blue and cadmium red into the wet sky wash.*

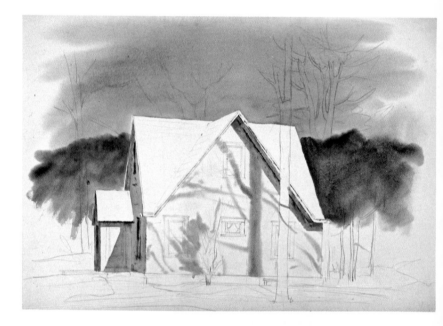

Step 5. *While the sky wash is still damp, I sponge in the large pine tree just to the right of the house with a mixture of sap green, burnt sienna, and cobalt blue. As this settles into the paper, I strengthen its value with sap green, more burnt sienna, and ink, applied with a sponge. Where the trunk of this tree passes in front of the purple mountain, I use a moist brush to lift out an area of the purple wash. Where I lifted out the purple value, I paint in the trunk and the branches of the tree with burnt sienna, cobalt blue, and black ink, and add texture to the bark with a No. 2 brush and India ink.*

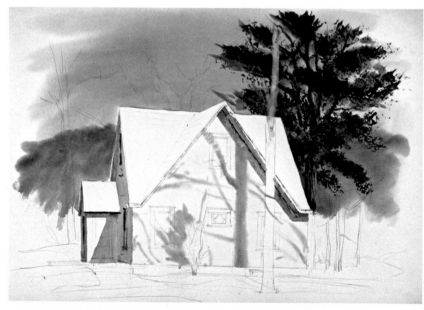

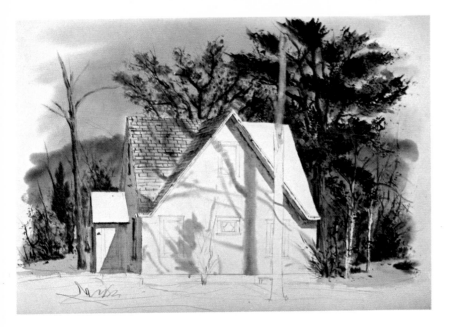

Step 6. *For this step, I protect the roof, both above the house and over the doorway, by covering those areas with light pieces of cardboard. Then I re-wet the sky and the mountain areas by blowing clear water on them from a fixative blower. While these areas are wet, I add the tree behind the house and the small trees on either side, first sponging in mixtures of sap green, burnt sienna, and cobalt blue, then brushing in the trunks with burnt sienna, cobalt blue, and black ink. Finally, I add a bit of texture to the trunks with India ink.*

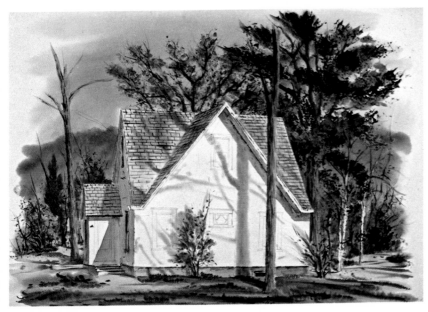

Step 7. *I wet the foreground with a sponge and clear water and wash in burnt sienna to indicate the ground. Then, with a fanned-out brush, I wash in sap green and raw sienna where I want to indicate grass. I wet the area next to the house where I've sketched the bush and paint in the bush with my foliage values. I paint in the trunk of the tree in front of the house with cobalt blue, burnt sienna, and ink and add some texture with a No. 2 brush and ink. I finish this step by painting the gray foundation of the house with a mixture of cobalt blue, burnt sienna, and a touch of cadmium red.*

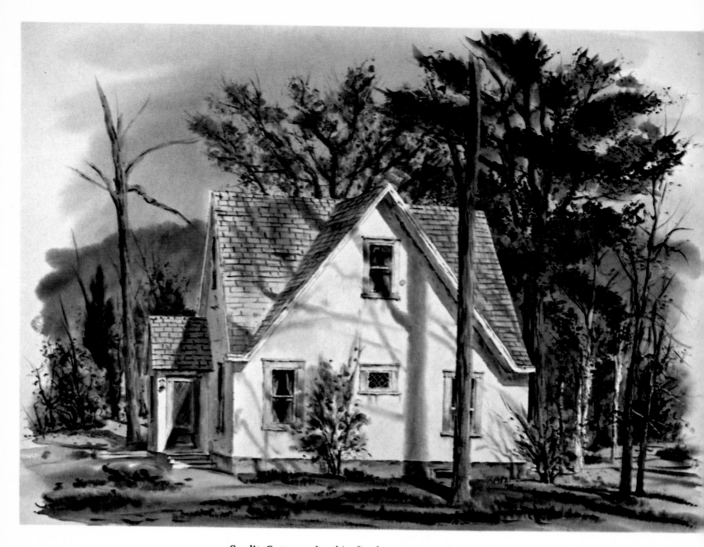

Sunlit Cottage. *In this final step, I gently wet the areas around the windows with a 1" flat brush and clear water and carefully paint the trim with tints of burnt sienna and cadmium red. To indicate the windowpanes, I use burnt sienna, raw sienna, and India ink. I follow the same procedure to indicate the trim and the glass in the door, wetting the cast shadow and strengthening it with more cadmium red, cobalt blue, and raw sienna, just before it dries.*

Here, you'll learn how to paint white houses in subtle gray values, against a backlit sky. I'll use cadmium red, permanent blue, cobalt blue, raw sienna, burnt sienna, raw umber, sap green, and black India ink. I'll use the same four brushes as for the last demonstration, natural sponges, and rough Arches pre-mounted watercolor board (22" x 30").

WOODEN HOUSE IN SUBTLE GRAYS

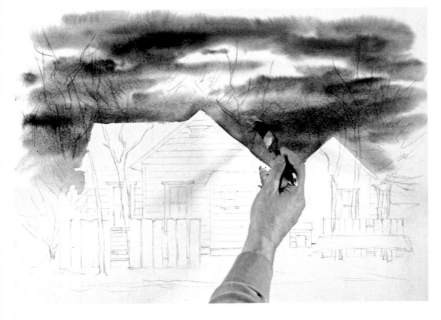

Step 1. *First, I double-wet the sky area with clear water, using a brush and then a sponge. With the 1" flat brush, I drop in pale tints of cadmium red and allow them to spread. Then I paint in dark clouds with mixtures of cobalt blue, permanent blue, and burnt sienna.*

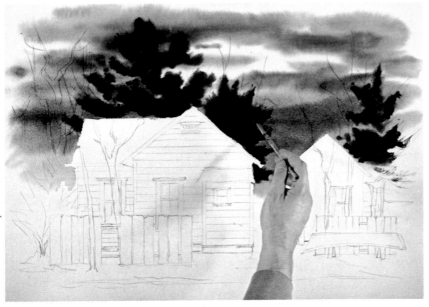

Step 2. *With a No. 6 brush loaded with sap green and cobalt blue, I begin painting pine trees into the wet sky. I strengthen these tree passages with black ink and burnt sienna. When the trees are nearly dry, I stipple the area lightly with the same colors, mixed with black ink and scooped up on a sponge, to add texture.*

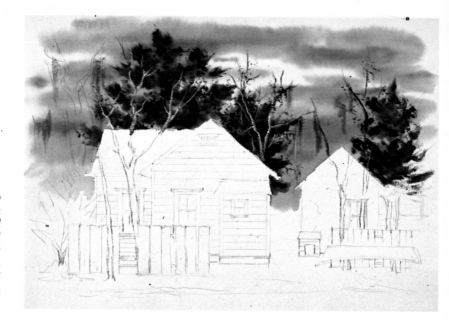

Step 3. *I add touches of raw umber to the damp sky wash to indicate moss in some of the trees. While the stippled mixtures in the trees are still damp, I use the handle of a brush to press out color where I want to indicate branches; when the colors dry completely, I use an X-Acto knife blade to scrape out more texture.*

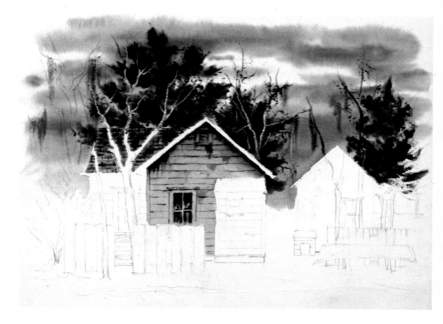

Step 4. *I carefully paint in the roof shingles wet-in-wet, using cadmium red and burnt sienna for the overall value, and adding the texture with a No. 2 brush and black ink. I paint the front part of the house with a mixture of cobalt blue, cadmium red, and raw sienna and the underside of the roof with cobalt blue and black India ink. I leave the entrance area blank for now. I wet the window areas and define them with burnt sienna and black ink. To indicate the wooden siding, I use black ink and a small No. 2 brush.*

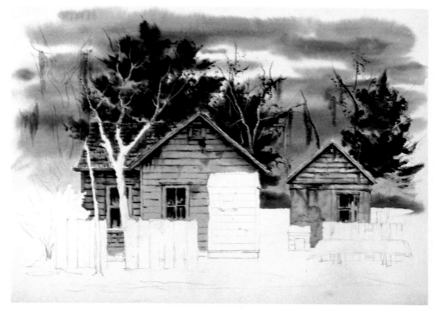

Step 5. *I paint in the front of the small building on the right, using the same procedure and colors I used in Step 4. Under the roofs, where they cast shadows on the walls of the buildings, I apply pure ink and allow it to bleed and run into the color on the walls. Then I give life to the gray areas with a few stains of burnt sienna. After wetting the horizon line with a brush and clear water, I paint the mountain with cobalt blue and cadmium red.*

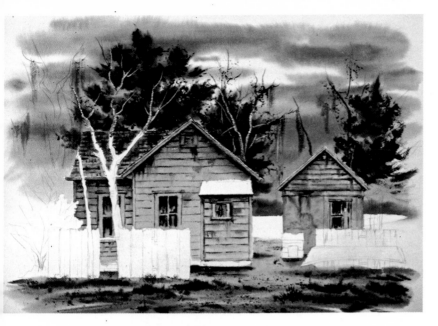

Step 6. *I paint the small entrance area next. Then I wet the foreground and paint it in with washes of raw sienna and burnt sienna mixed with cobalt blue and permanent blue. I brush sap green and black ink into the grass for texture. Then I spatter the foreground with dark colors and leave it to dry.*

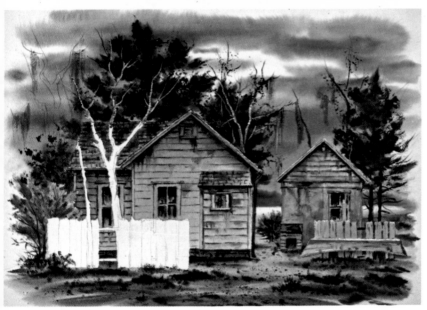

Step 7. *I paint the fence and the boat, using the colors I used on the house. I re-wet the bush areas and use a sponge loaded with dark color and ink to add the darker bushes. I paint and stipple in the lighter green bush, using a No. 6 brush.*

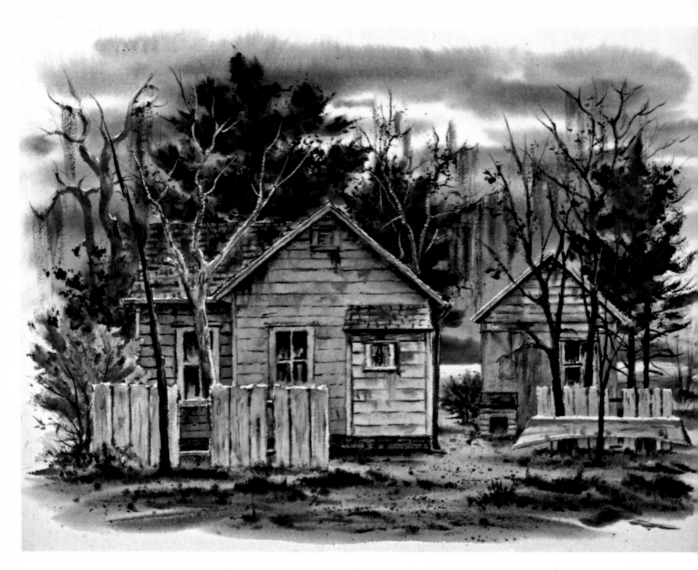

Down Georgia Way. *In this last step, I paint in the rest of the fence with warm, reflected light on the bottom. I paint in the rest of the trees and add more Spanish moss to achieve a better balance.*

This picture is loaded with summer greens, and I'll show you how to treat them with a variety of textures, as well as how to vary colors to break up monotony. I'll paint a bright, sunny morning scene, with the sunlight coming from the left. I'll use a sheet of 300 lb. Arches cold-pressed paper, stretched on a 3/4″ plywood board; burnt sienna, cobalt blue, raw sienna, cadmium red, sap green, and India ink; and the usual four brushes and natural sponges.

CLAPBOARD HOUSE IN SUNLIGHT AND SHADOW

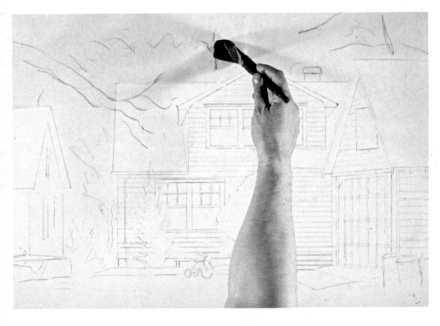

Step 1. *To begin, I wet the entire area above and between the houses with clear water.*

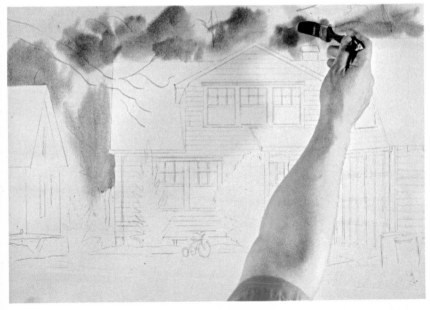

Step 2. *I paint raw sienna and sap green into this wet area, using a 1″ flat brush. I add touches of burnt sienna mixed with the same colors wet-in-wet to form an abstract pattern.*

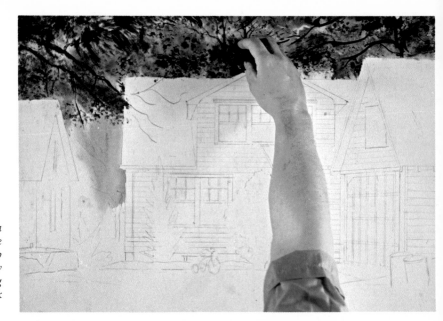

Step 3. *I paint some branches, using a No. 6 round brush loaded with pure black ink. I moisten a sponge and dip it into an undiluted mixture of raw sienna and sap green. After stippling in this mixture, I stipple in black ink with a clean sponge.*

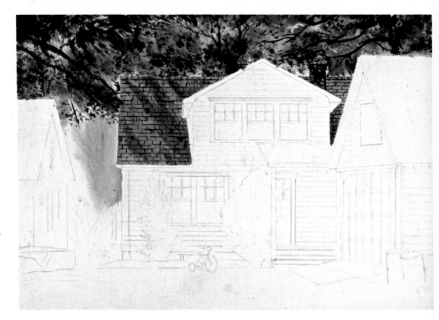

Step 4. *When this top area is dry, I paint in the roof, using medium-value washes of raw sienna, cadmium red, and cobalt blue; and I strengthen the area with strong shadow washes of cobalt blue and cadmium red. I use a No. 2 brush and ink for shingle textures while the washes are still wet, and paint the chimney in cadmium red and black ink.*

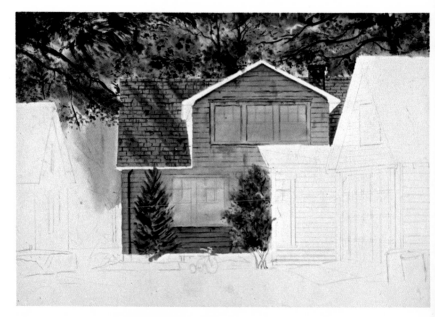

Step 5. *I wet the front of the central house with clear water, flood in cobalt blue with touches of cadmium red and burnt sienna, and warm this value up with raw sienna. I add the bushes next, using the procedure I used for the trees in Steps 1, 2, and 3. Then I add inklines for a clapboard effect.*

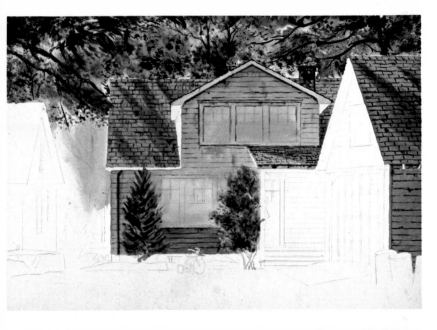

Step 6. *I use the same wet-in-wet technique and the same colors that I used in Steps 4 and 5 to render the roof and the side of the garage.*

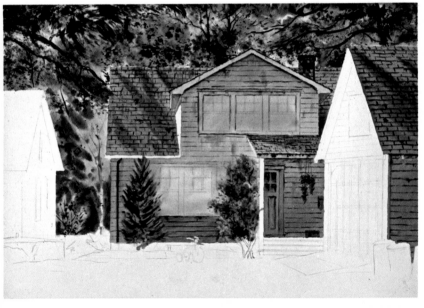

Step 7. *To paint the doorway area, I use cobalt blue with touches of burnt sienna and cadmium red, and I warm up the value with raw sienna. With a small brush, I add touches of sap green and cadmium red wet-in-wet to indicate the hanging plant.*

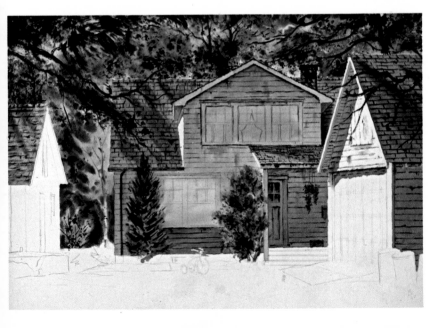

Step 8. *Using the colors and techniques I used in Steps 2 and 3, I extend some branches over the roof of the central cottage and the roof of the garage. Then I use cobalt blue and raw sienna to indicate the cast shadows over the garage door and under the garage roof.*

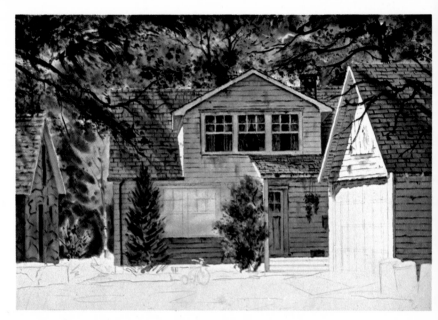

Step 9. *I finish the cottage on the left, using sap green in a gray mixture of cobalt blue, cadmium red, and burnt sienna. I re-wet and paint in the window and suggest curtains with raw sienna and black ink.*

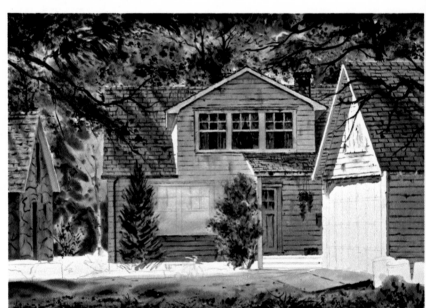

Step 10. *I wet the foreground and lay in washes of burnt sienna and raw sienna first, followed by cobalt blue with burnt sienna for shadows, and then more of the same colors mixed with ink. I load a sponge with the same colors, undiluted, then add ink, and stipple in texture.*

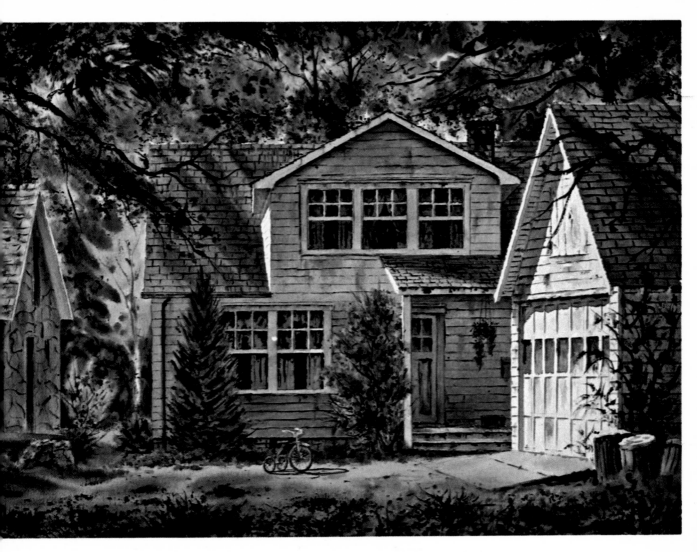

Kemple House. *Finally, I complete the windows, using raw sienna and ink. I paint in the little bicycle with pale tints of raw sienna, burnt sienna, and cadmium red, and add accents with black ink. I paint the garbage cans with raw sienna, cobalt blue, and burnt sienna, indicating the corrugated texture with ink, and adding the bush behind them with my usual green mixture. I paint the garage doors with cobalt blue, burnt sienna, raw sienna, and ink.*

DEMONSTRATION 17

PENNSYLVANIA FARM IN SNOW

In this demonstration, I'll discuss the techniques you can use to paint snow. When you're using transparent watercolors, you can leave your white paper blank where you want to indicate snow; the only values you'll need to paint in will be for the objects that are not completely covered with snow, and for the shadow areas on the snow.

As you'll see in Steps 10 and 11, an artist isn't necessarily confined to his original idea for a painting. At the end of Step 10, the painting looked as I had originally intended. But I later decided to improve the composition by adding new elements.

I'll use a 22″ x 30″ sheet of cold-pressed 300 lb. Arches paper; the usual brushes and sponges; permanent blue, cobalt blue, burnt sienna, raw sienna, raw umber, sap green, cadmium red, cadmium orange, and black India ink.

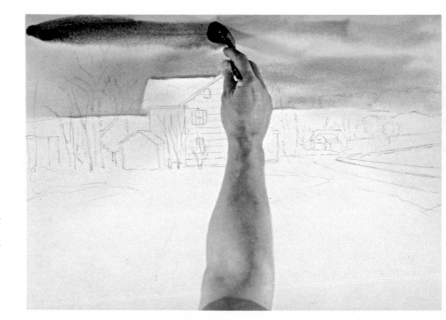

Step 1. *First, I double-wet the top of the paper around the buildings with clear water and brush in mixtures of burnt sienna and raw sienna unevenly. Then I work cloud effects into the wet washes with mixtures of burnt sienna, permanent blue, and cobalt blue.*

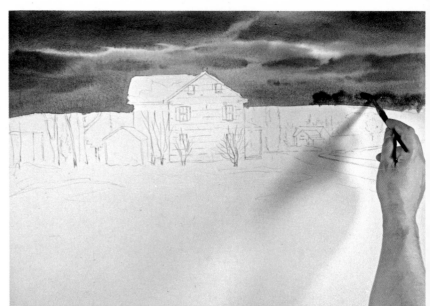

Step 2. *When the clouds are complete, just before the sky wash is dry, I add the trees on the distant hill to the right, using a No. 6 brush loaded with burnt sienna, raw umber, cobalt blue, and ink.*

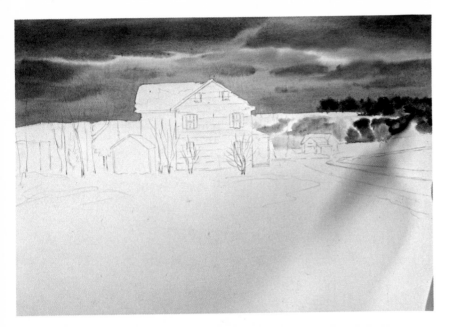

Step 3. *I wet the hill to the right, behind the house, with clear water and wash in a tint of raw umber and cadmium orange. I paint the larger trees on the hill next, applying burnt sienna, cobalt blue, and cadmium red, with a No. 6 brush.*

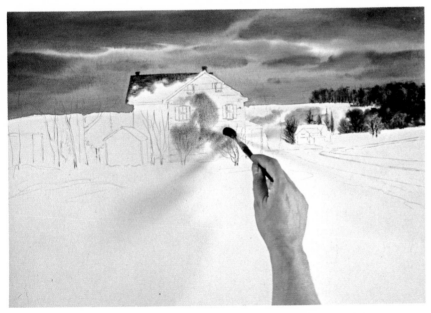

Step 4. *I complete the hill and the trees in back of the distant barn, using the same techniques and colors I used in Step 3. I wet the roof of the house with clear water and wash in texture with burnt sienna and raw sienna mixed with ink, leaving most of the paper white to indicate snow. I wet the face of the building and flood in mixtures of cobalt blue and cadmium red with a No. 6 brush.*

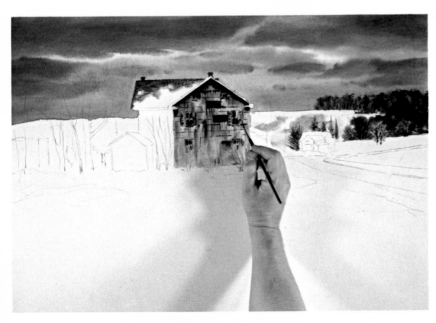

Step 5. *I paint burnt sienna and India ink into the wet purple basewash on the house. Then, with black ink, I paint the window wet-in-wet and suggest the wood siding.*

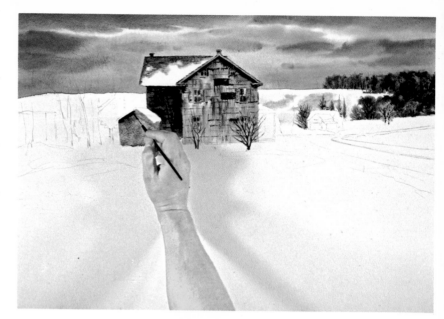

Step 6. *I wash in a dark mixture of cobalt blue and burnt sienna on the deep shadow side of the house and add suggestions of windows in the shadow with black ink and a No. 2 brush. I also indicate the bare bushes in front of the house and near the shadow side with black ink, wash in the shed near the house with raw sienna, burnt sienna, and cobalt blue, and add shadow under the roof with black ink. I indicate texture and snow on this roof as I did on the roof of the house.*

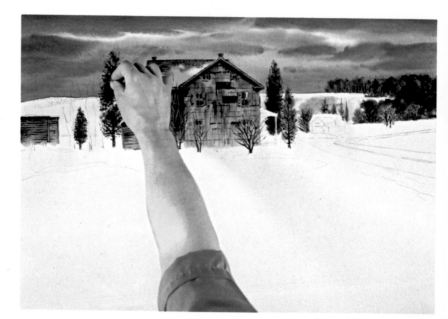

Step 7. *I paint the other shed in the same manner and stipple in the trees with a sponge loaded with sap green, burnt sienna, and black ink.*

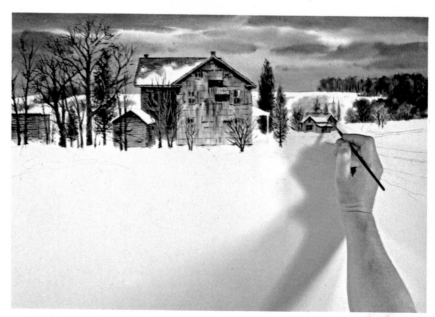

Step 8. *I paint in the larger trees with permanent blue, burnt sienna, and India ink; then I paint the barn in the distance with cadmium red, cobalt blue, and touches of ink, leaving "snow" on the roof.*

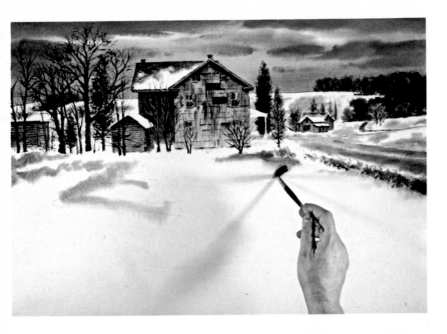

Step 9. *I paint the road, using cobalt blue, cadmium red, and a touch of sap green. The tufts of grass along the road are next: I wet the entire foreground and wash in raw sienna and burnt sienna with a No. 6 round brush.*

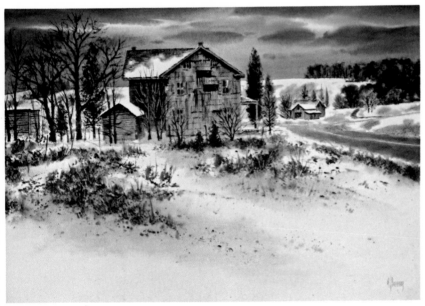

Step 10. *I load a sponge with raw umber and ink and lightly stipple in some shrubbery. I paint wet-in-wet snow shadows in the field with a blue-gray mixture, then stipple again with raw umber and ink on the sponge. Now comes some spatter treatment. For this, I use some of the dark colors I have on my pallette. The painting could be considered "finished" at this point, so I'll live with it this way overnight before I decide whether or not to continue.*

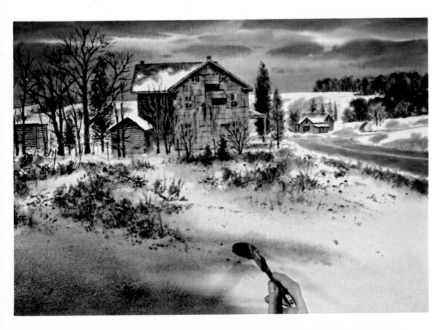

Step 11. *Having decided to do some further work on the "finished" painting, I re-wet the entire foreground and put in dark shadows of permanent blue, cobalt blue, and burnt sienna, with a 1" flat brush.*

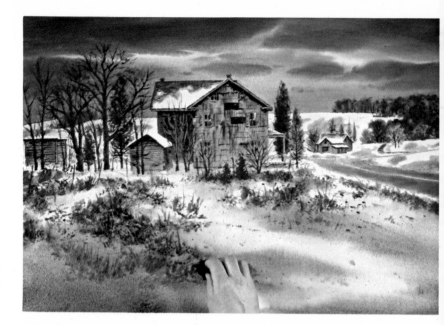

Step 12. *I continue to fill in the foreground, stippling, fanning the brush, and adding some wild, haphazard strokes. I lift out and sponge out some areas to begin creating rock effects, and leave the painting to dry.*

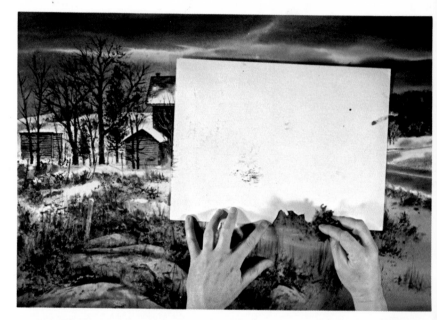

Step 13. *Now I protect the painting with masks cut from heavy paper as I sponge out crisp edges to create "rock" effects. To balance the composition, I add a fence post by masking the area with tape, sponging out the old color, and painting in a mixture of cobalt blue and raw sienna.*

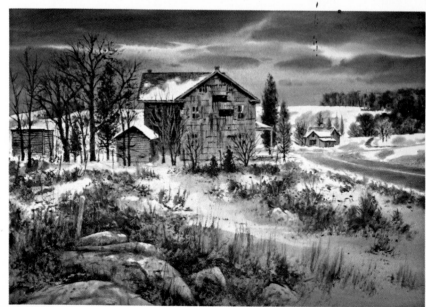

Step 14. *I scrape and hack out some areas on the rocks with a sharp blade and use the electric eraser here and there. Then I fill in more color along with some drybrush and scumbling. (By scumbling, I mean a variety of techniques which I use rather randomly to create texture. These include drybrush, spattering, stippling, dragging the brush through the paint on the paper, etc.)*

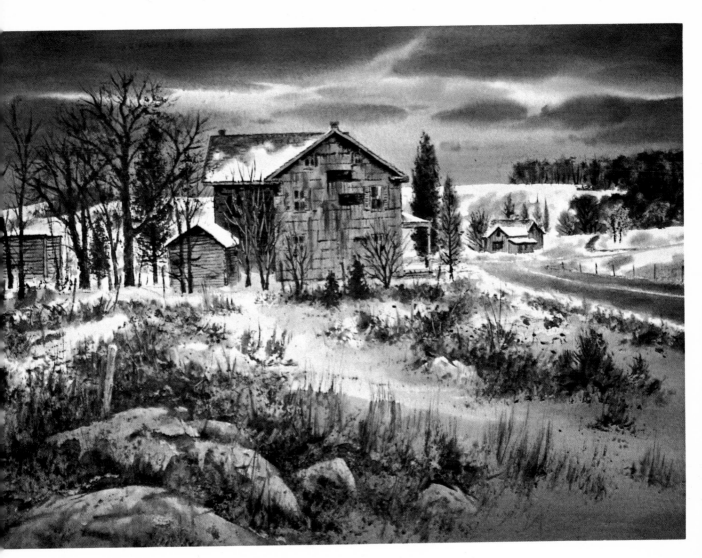

Pennsylvania, March. *In this final step, I add the fence posts on the right, along the road, because I feel that area needs a few more vertical lines to tie it together. There are still too many horizontal lines converging on each other in the rocks, so I change the structure of the rocks in the lower left portion of the picture. I scrape out part of the horizontal division between the rocks with a knife blade and an eraser and add more of the same color and some drybrush to create one unbroken area of rock. Then I call a final halt.*

DEMONSTRATION 18

FRONT PORCH WITH FAÇADE

Now, we'll deal with painting large masses of green around a busy façade of balustrades and deep-shadowed windows. The colors will be burnt sienna, cobalt blue, raw sienna, cadmium red, cadmium orange, sap green, and black ink. I'll use the same brushes and natural sponges, and a rough sheet of Arches 300 lb. watercolor paper, soaked and stretched on a 3/4″ plywood board.

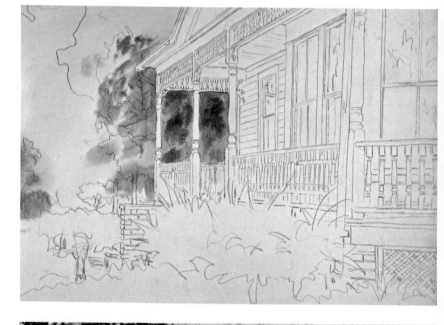

Step 1. *I wet the sky and the area between the porch columns and wash them in with a pale mixture of burnt sienna and raw sienna. Then I use a mixture of burnt sienna, raw sienna, and a touch of cobalt blue and cadmium red for the distant trees. To suggest the nearer bushes, I paint in some raw sienna and sap green.*

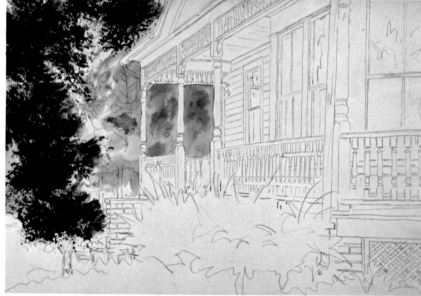

Step 2. *While this is still wet, I paint in cobalt blue and raw sienna with a No. 10 brush, as an underwash for the foliage. Then I use the sponge technique, with sap green, burnt sienna and cobalt blue, and follow it with a light stippling of sponge and pure ink, to indicate the foliage.*

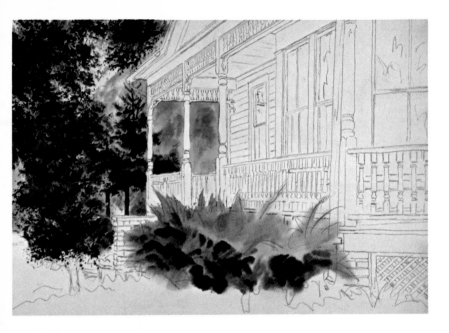

Step 3. *In the background, I add more texture and trees. I wet the large bush in the foreground with clear water and paint sap green and raw sienna wet-in-wet and strengthen it with sap green, burnt sienna, and ink.*

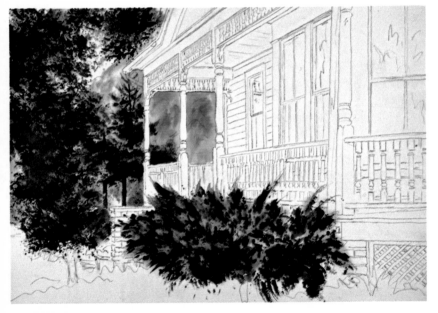

Step 4. *I sponge-stipple the bush in the foreground with the same colors and black ink. When this is nearly dry, I brush in flicks of cadmium orange with a No. 6 brush, to add color vibration and vigor to the bush.*

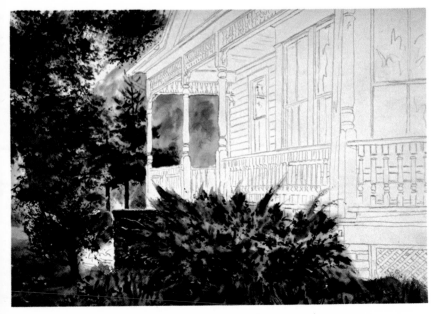

Step 5. *I wet the foreground with clear water and brush in washes of raw sienna and sap green. I put in deep mixtures of cobalt blue, sap green, and raw sienna; then I stroke in sap green and ink to complete the major area. When this is just about dry, I dab in cadmium orange with a small brush, to add interest. I put in the wall along the brick staircase with cadmium red, cobalt blue, and ink, and scrape some branches out of the bush with a sharp blade.*

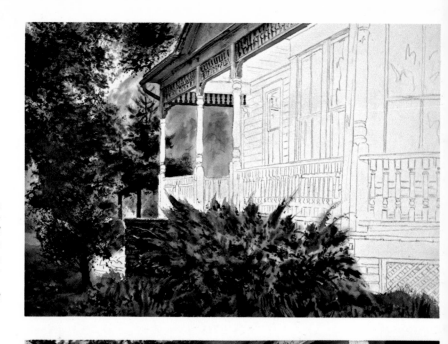

Step 6. *I wet the area above the porch and paint it wet-in-wet with raw sienna, cadmium red, cobalt blue, and ink. Then I fill in the sky between the upper balusters, matching it up with the distance area of haze. When this section is dry, I paint in the balusters, using cobalt blue, cadmium red, and raw sienna.*

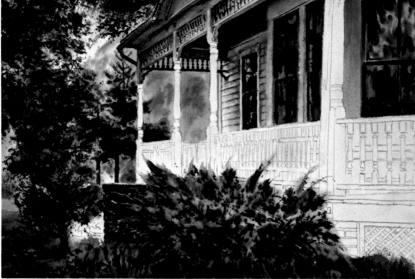

Step 7. *I wet the window and door on the house proper with clear water and paint in a medium wash of cobalt blue and raw sienna. While this wash is still damp, I paint into it deep mixtures of cobalt blue, sap green, burnt sienna, and ink. Then I paint the ceiling in shadow under the roof of the porch, using deep washes of cobalt blue, cadmium red, and raw sienna, with touches of ink in the far corners.*

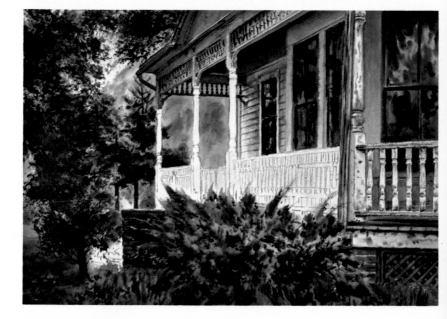

Step 8. *Wetting and working on each area individually with a small brush, I paint the drainpipe with cobalt blue and burnt sienna; the balusters with cadmium red, cobalt blue, and raw sienna; and the latticework with sap green, cobalt blue, burnt sienna, and ink. For the mortar joints, I brush in a pale underwash of cobalt blue and raw sienna; then I render the bricks with cadmium red, cobalt blue, and a touch of ink.*

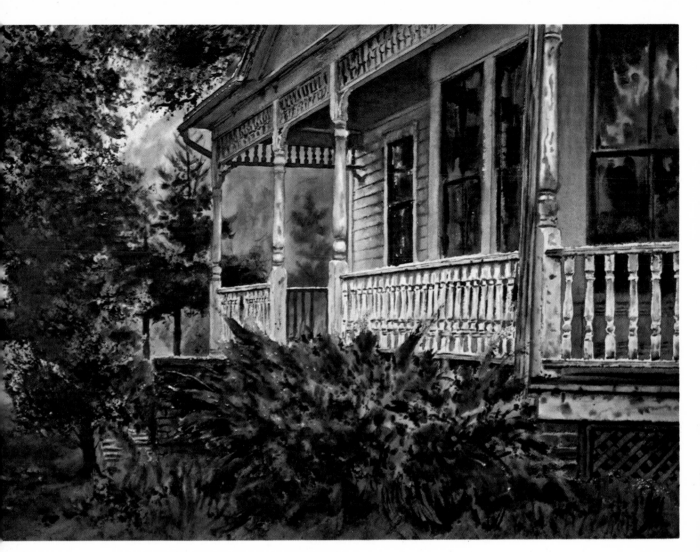

Yesterday. *Finally, I use the same pick and peck procedure on the rest of the porch—wetting each baluster and railing separately and introducing bits of color. I work a little drybrush and ink into the small, semi-wet areas, and the picture seems complete. Sometimes, a picture will need a second wash to bring it together, but this picture came off the first time and didn't need any retouching.*

DEMONSTRATION 19

CONCRETE BUNKER IN SNOW

This particular subject intrigued me, with the warm-hued rust stains of the concrete bunker contrasting against the cold blue-grays of the snow.

My palette will consist of burnt sienna, raw sienna, burnt umber, cadmium red, cadmium orange, sap green, cobalt blue, and black ink. I'll use the same tools and a sheet of Arches 300 lb. cold-pressed paper, stretched and ready to go.

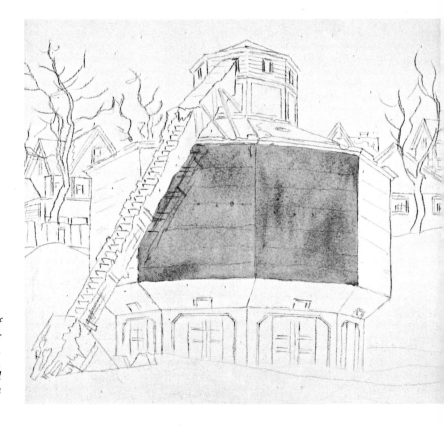

Step 1. *I wet the center two sections of the octagonal bunker with clear water and float in burnt sienna, raw sienna, and cobalt blue with a flat 1" brush, using uneven strokes so the warm and cool colors will work against each other.*

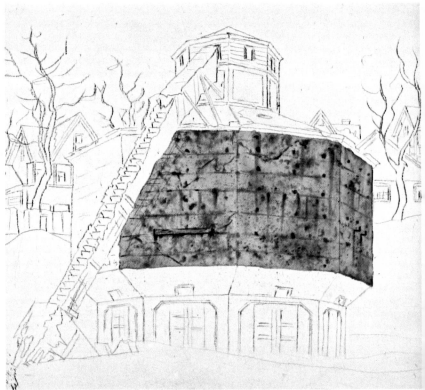

Step 2. *I let this dry. Then I wet and paint the right section in the same way and let it dry thoroughly. I re-wet the entire area very carefully with a 1" flat brush and clear water and spatter in rust stains, textures, and pit marks with cobalt blue, burnt sienna, raw sienna, and ink, as I try to achieve the effect of old concrete. By letting the first washes dry, I can create a heavier texture and feeling than I can by adding the effects wet-in-wet.*

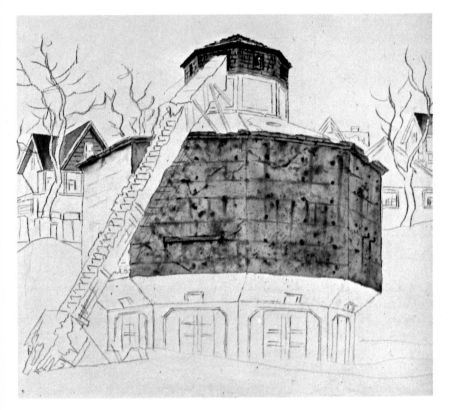

Step 3. *I paint in the old wooden top and roof of the bunker with cadmium red and cobalt blue and add black ink for texture. With the same colors, I paint the housetops. I use a lighter mixture of raw sienna and burnt sienna on the house in back and texture it with ink.*

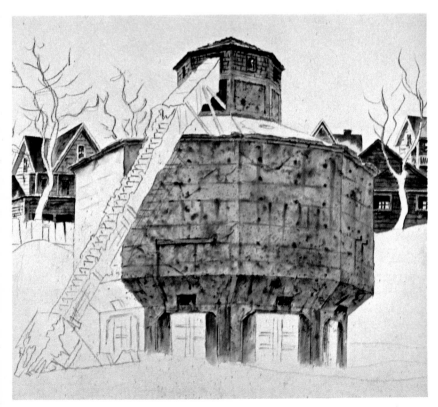

Step 4. *I use the same colors that I used in Steps 1 and 2 on the rest of the concrete, this time working them in directly, wet-in-wet, instead of letting the first wash dry. I paint in more housetops and use burnt umber and black ink to paint the old garage on the right rear. I use burnt sienna and cadmium orange on the small shed in the left rear.*

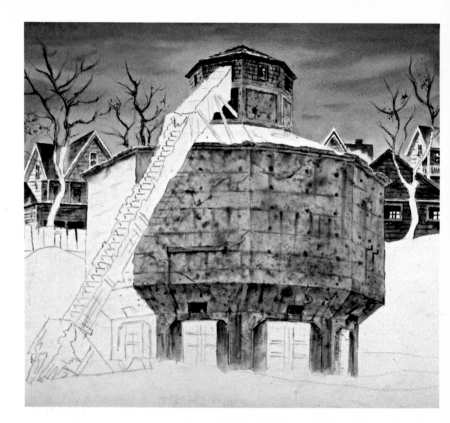

Step 5. *I wet the sky area with clear water and paint in cobalt blue and a light touch of sap green with a 1" flat brush. When this wash settles into the paper, I use burnt sienna and burnt umber mixed with cobalt blue to introduce darker sky washes. While the sky is still moist, I paint in the top branches of the trees with almost-dry burnt sienna, raw sienna, and ink and stipple with raw sienna and raw umber.*

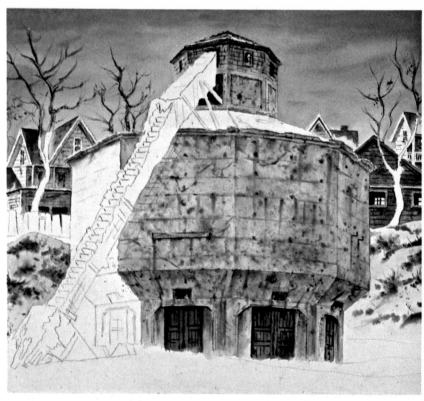

Step 6. *I paint in the old, faded wooden doors next, using a No. 6 round brush and sap green, burnt sienna, and cobalt blue and texture them with India ink. I wash in the snowbanks in the rear with cobalt blue and a touch of burnt umber and texture them by painting burnt sienna, raw sienna, and black ink into them wet-in-wet with a No. 6 brush.*

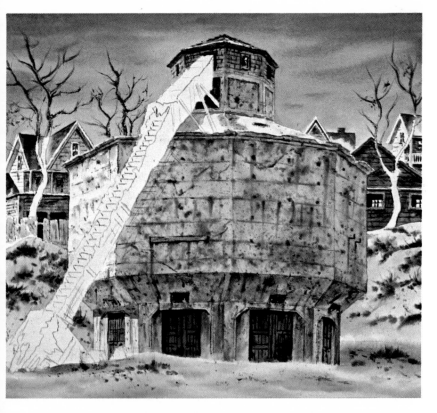

Step 7. *I sponge the foreground with clear water and flood in washes of cobalt blue mixed with a touch of raw sienna on a 1" flat brush. While this is still wet, I texture the washes with burnt sienna and black ink. I paint the sunlit side of the bunker with touches of burnt sienna and raw sienna and stipple it lightly with ink. Then I paint the doors in a pale mixture of the values I used in Step 6 and add the dark cast shadow. I mix a very pale purple value, add a touch of raw sienna for warmth, and work it into the wooden fence, along with a touch of ink.*

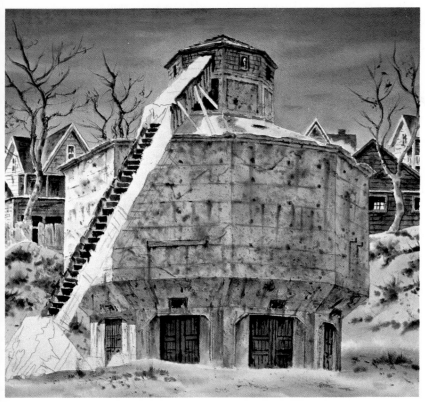

Step 8. *I work on the old metal conveyor belt next, using cobalt blue and cadmium red. I work on it in sections, laying a flat purple wash first, letting it dry, and working in a deeper purple value dry on top. Then I complete the trees, using the same colors and techniques I used in Step 5.*

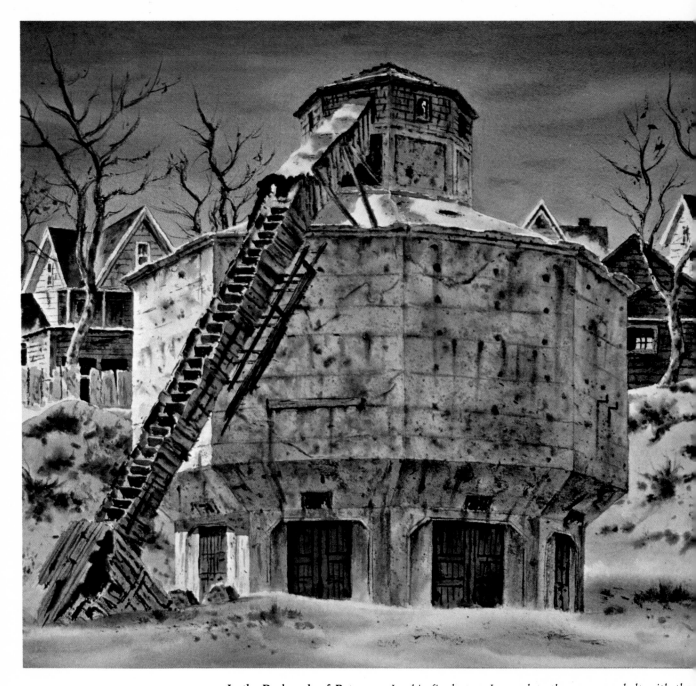

In the Backyards of Paterson. *In this final step, I complete the conveyor belt with the same approach and the same colors, using a little black ink to strengthen and texture the broken wood stairs. With the same colors again, I paint the decayed loading bin of corrugated metal and the wooden areas wet-in-wet and indicate the little concrete footing that once held some conveyor supports.*

This picture interested me because more than two-thirds of it is in shadow. I'll keep most of the shadow area in cool tones, and let sunlight warm the treetops and the small area of stone above the stairs. I'll use a sheet of 300 lb. Arches cold-pressed paper and the usual tools. My palette will consist of cadmium red, burnt sienna, cobalt blue, permanent blue, raw sienna, raw umber, sap green, and black India ink.

STONE ARCHES IN SHADOW

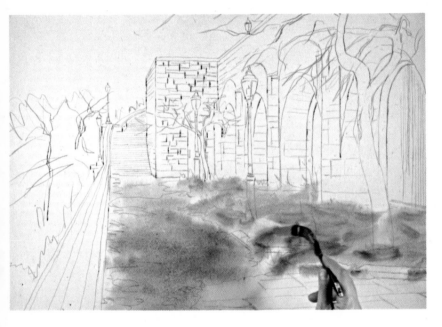

Step 1. *I double-wet the entire ground area with clear water and float in mixtures of cobalt blue, cadmium red, and burnt sienna, unevenly, with a 1" flat brush. Adjacent to this wet area, I brush in burnt sienna and raw sienna to indicate the growth at the right.*

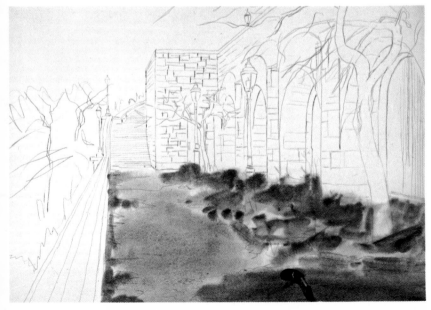

Step 2. *I brush cadmium red, burnt sienna, and raw umber into the base-wash. As this settles and spreads a little, I apply the same mixture again to deepen the washes.*

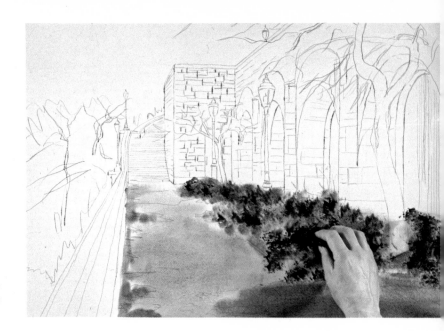

Step 3. *For texture, I stipple in raw umber, burnt sienna, and black ink with a sponge.*

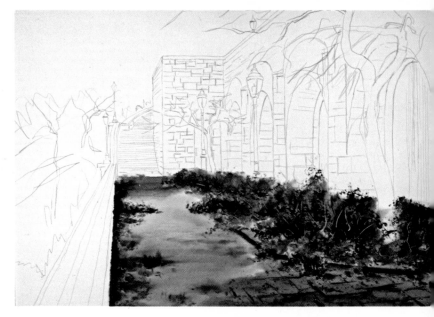

Step 4. *Just before this conglomeration is dry, I suggest pavement stones by applying thick mixtures of the colors I used in Step 2, mixed with black ink on a brush; and I use some spatter technique. Then I press out the small branches with the back end of a small brush handle and let the area dry.*

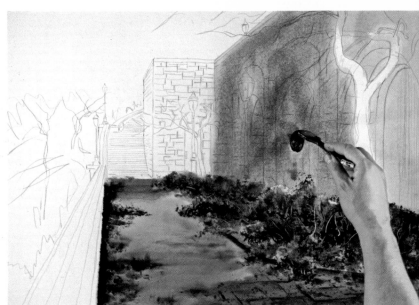

Step 5. *I double-wet the area of the arches, leaving the tree dry, and flood in mixtures of raw sienna and raw umber mixed with cobalt blue, using a 1" flat brush.*

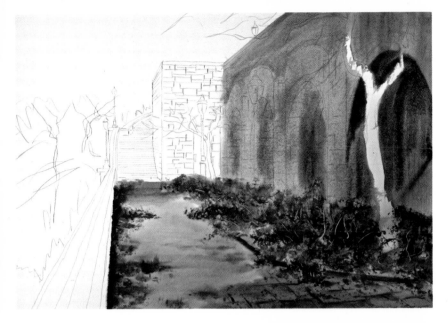

Step 6. *I add burnt sienna above the arches and paint the arch areas with mixtures of permanent blue, cobalt blue, and burnt sienna with a No. 6 brush, keeping the colors on the cool side.*

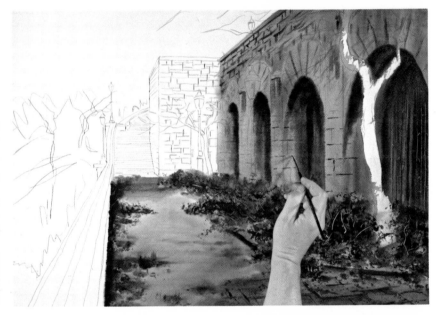

Step 7. *I delineate the bricks around the arches with black ink and suggest mortar joints with a thick mixture of burnt sienna and ink, using a No. 2 brush.*

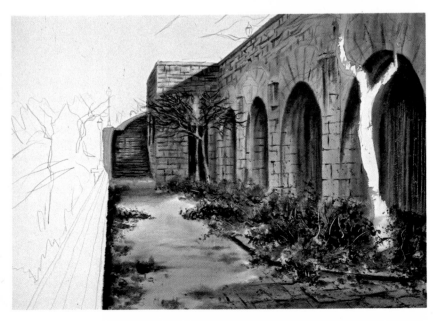

Step 8. *I paint the back wall and stairs wet-in-wet with the same colors and techniques that I used above the arches. Then I swish in a sponge loaded with burnt sienna and burnt umber for the trees in the rear, press out some branches with a brush handle, and define them with strokes of black ink to create the effect of branches.*

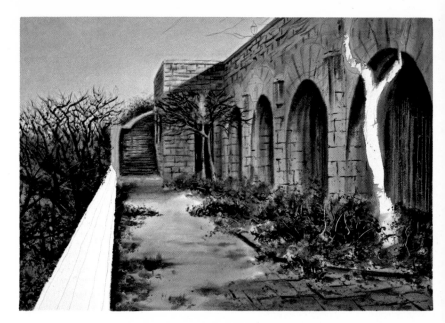

Step 9. *I wet the sky area and the entire left side of the painting with a sponge and clear water. I paint in a pale tint of cobalt blue and raw sienna for the sky. Then I paint and sponge in deep colors of raw umber, raw sienna, and cobalt blue, with a bit of sap green, to suggest a mass of trees and bushes. Again, I stipple this area lightly with ink and dark color.*

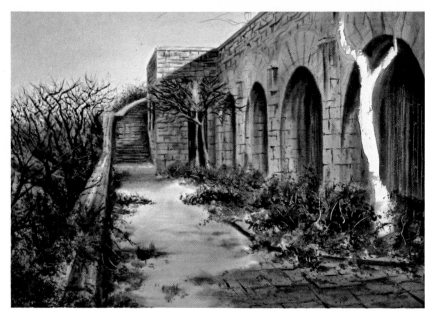

Step 10. *Using the same colors that I used on the walls, I paint in the concrete railing and let it dry. Then I rewet this area with a fixative sprayer and clear water. With a sponge, I stipple raw umber, burnt sienna, permanent blue, and black ink over the concrete wall to break the straight line and add interest. I press out a few branches with the end of the brush handle.*

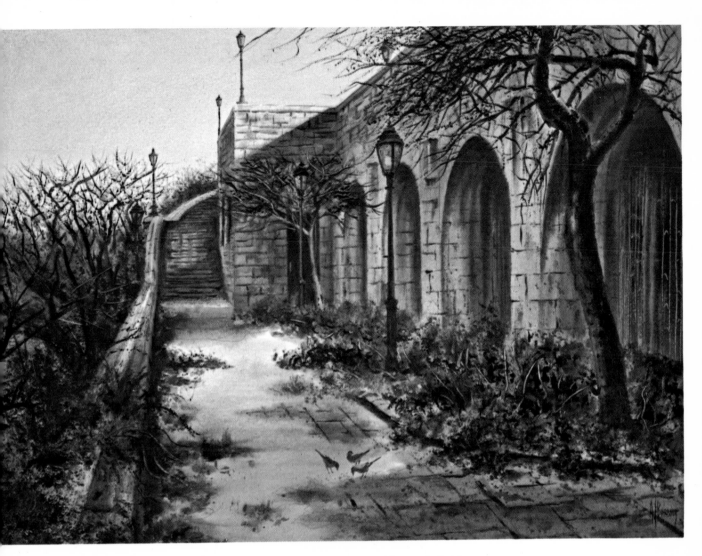

Solitude. *Finally, I complete the tree. For the trunk, I use permanent blue, cobalt blue, and touches of cadmium red, raw sienna, and ink, on the No. 10 round brush; I use cobalt blue, burnt sienna, and ink on the No. 6 brush for the branches.*

DEMONSTRATION 21

NEW YORK STREET IN LATE AFTERNOON

In this picture, I want to capture the late afternoon light that hits the tops of the buildings while the rest of the scene is in shadow. Again, I'll keep the shadow values cool and let the sunlight warm up the areas it hits.

I'll use a sheet of Arches 300 lb. cold-pressed paper; raw sienna, burnt sienna, cobalt blue, permanent blue, cadmium red, sap green, cadmium yellow, and black India ink; and the same brushes and sponges, as well as a 1″ flat brush, and a No. 10 round brush.

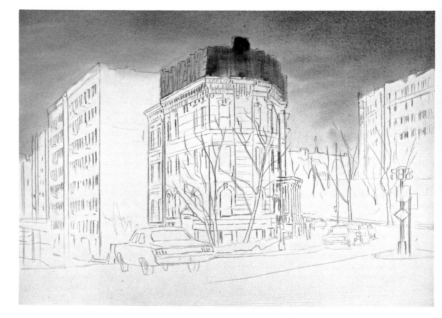

Step 1. *I wet the complete sky area and the top of the center building with clear water and flood in raw sienna with a 1″ flat brush. Then I brush in cobalt blue and a touch of burnt sienna wet-in-wet, for a late afternoon sky. While this is still damp, I attack the roof of the building. I paint in permanent blue and cobalt blue mixed with raw sienna on a small No. 6 brush, and let the edge of the roof bleed slightly into the sky. Then I lightly touch in some burnt sienna and let the area dry.*

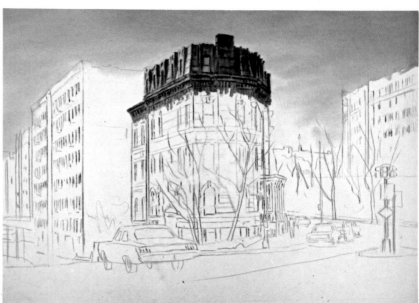

Step 2. *I re-wet the top of the building and develop it further, first applying the same colors wet-in-wet, and then adding India ink with a brush.*

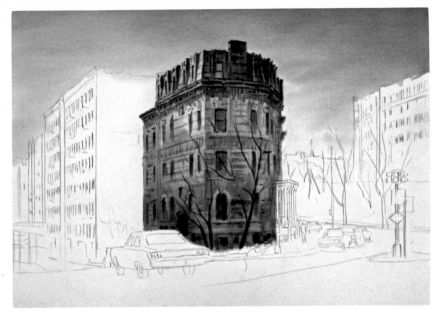

Step 3. *I wet the rest of the building with water and flood in raw sienna throughout with a 1" flat brush, adding cobalt blue with a touch of permanent blue to the wet wash in the shadow area. To designate the windows and ornamentation, I work in burnt sienna and permanent blue, with a bit of cobalt blue, and develop the area further with ink. To paint the main tree structure, I use a No. 6 brush and cobalt blue mixed with ink and touches of burnt sienna.*

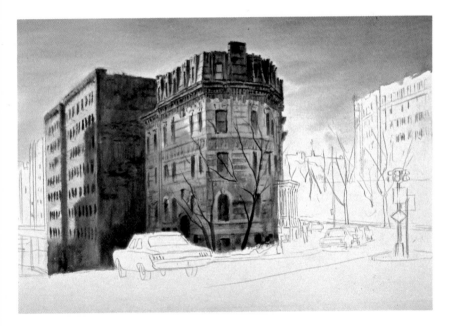

Step 4. *With clear water, I now wet part of the sky and the building on the left and wash in burnt sienna and raw sienna. When this settles, I use a bit of permanent blue and cobalt blue mixed with black ink to render the windows and the deep shadows; I put cadmium red in wet on the shadow side of the building to create the effect of old brick.*

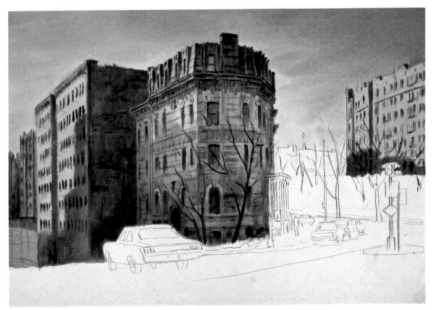

Step 5. *At this point, I re-wet the area at the extreme right with a soft 1" flat brush and water, and float in burnt sienna and raw sienna to indicate the building. When this settles into the paper a bit, I add a dark shadow to the wash with burnt sienna, cobalt blue, and permanent blue. I suggest the windows with the same colors. Then I wet the area on the far left and paint in the distant buildings.*

NEW YORK STREET IN LATE AFTERNOON 91

Step 6. *I wet the bank of earth at the right and paint in sap green and touches of burnt sienna, permanent blue, and cobalt blue with a No. 6 brush. I also paint the building in the distance with the colors I used in Step 5, adding a touch of cadmium red at the top. I stipple in the rest of the trees with burnt sienna on a sponge. Then I paint the tree trunks and branches with a thick, deep mixture of cobalt blue, permanent blue, and ink.*

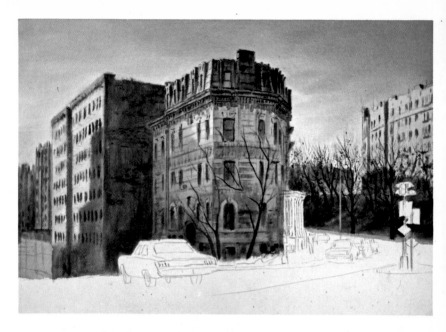

Step 7. *I wet the foreground area and paint in cobalt blue, burnt sienna, and raw sienna. I paint in the lower section of buildings on the left side, and the lower right section of the central building, with permanent blue, cobalt blue, burnt sienna, and black ink.*

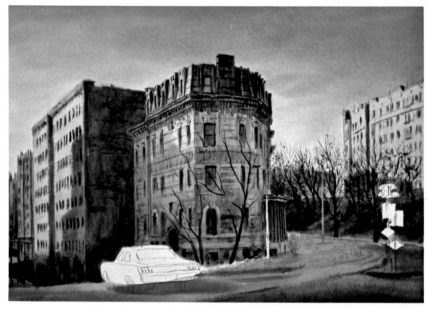

Step 8. *I paint in the large car with raw sienna, cobalt blue, and burnt sienna, using ink and color for the dark windows and the detail. Then I paint in the smaller cars on the right, using cadmium red, sap green, and ink directly over the dry foreground.*

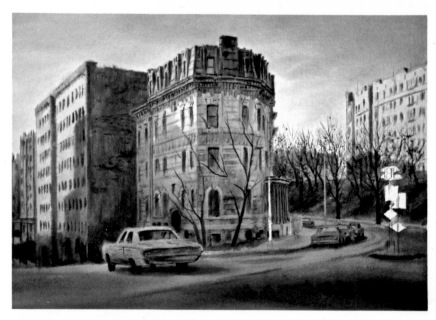

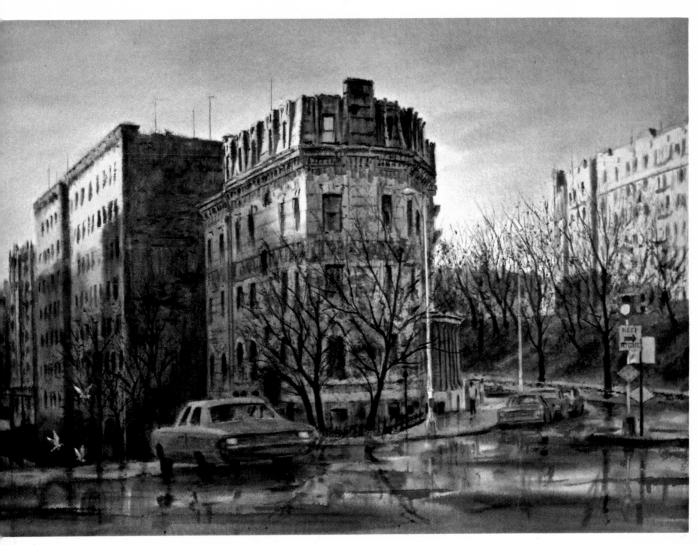

New York Street Scene. *I'm disappointed with the last two stages; the picture doesn't seem to work, and the car stands out like a sore thumb. So, I sponge out the whole foreground area with clear water and quickly paint wet-in-wet reflections in the street, using a 1" flat brush and a No. 6 round brush loaded with cobalt blue, sap green, and touches of cadmium red. For the reflection of the car, I use raw sienna. The picture is being rescued. I tone down the car value with permanent blue and paint the figure in yellow. After this, I play with the picture, making subtle, minor changes: inserting birds, developing the existing trees, and adding new trees and textures, until the picture seems complete.*

DEMONSTRATION 22

MONUMENT IN EARLY MORNING

Although I've been passing by this Soldiers' and Sailors' Monument all my life, usually in the middle of the day, I stopped cold when I saw it in the early light of a November morning; I had to paint it that way. My colors will be raw umber, burnt umber, sap green, burnt sienna, permanent blue, cobalt blue, and cadmium red, plus black India ink. I'll use the usual sponges and brushes, along with a stretched sheet of Arches 300 lb. watercolor paper.

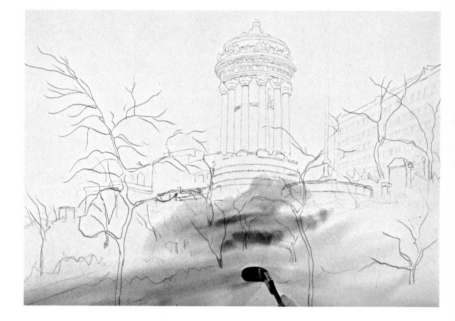

Step 1. *I sponge the entire bottom half of the sheet with clear water, spread in large washes of burnt sienna, sap green, and raw umber, and brush them into the wet paper with a 1" flat brush.*

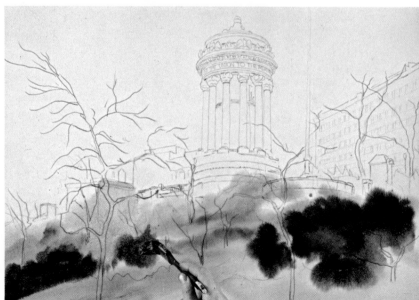

Step 2. *I add more burnt sienna for the distant trees and introduce a deep mixture of permanent blue, cobalt blue, and raw umber into the washes to start rendering some of the closer bushes and trees.*

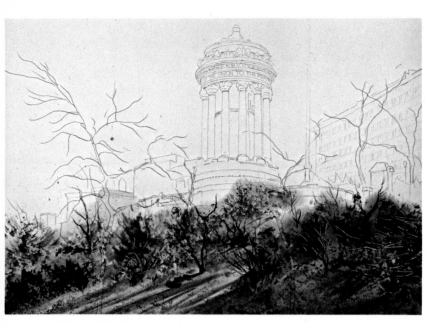

Step 3. *I paint in subtle but strong mixtures of sap green, raw umber, and ink with the No. 10 round brush to indicate the streaks of sunlight and shadows. Then I stipple flicks of burnt sienna and ink into this area with sponges. I brush in strokes of pure ink for branches and press out flickering lights with the back of a brush handle. I pull the foreground together with more stippling, using a sponge and dark paint.*

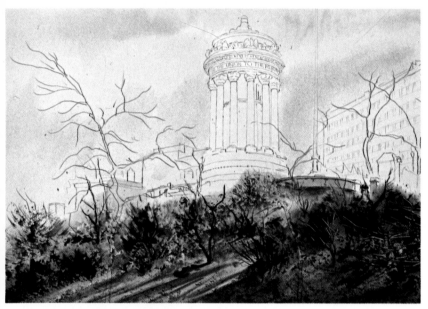

Step 4. *I paint in part of the circular platform with cadmium red and cobalt blue. Then I double-wet the sky area with clear water and flood in pale, soft washes of pure burnt sienna.*

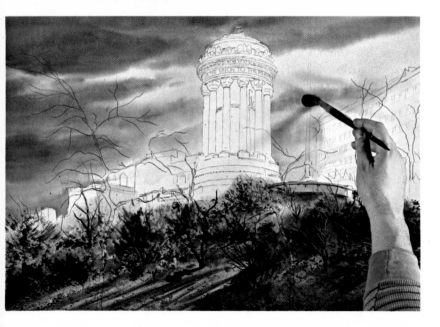

Step 5. *When these washes settle into the paper, I mix cobalt blue and a touch of permanent blue with burnt umber and "waft" the large clouds into place with a 1" flat brush.*

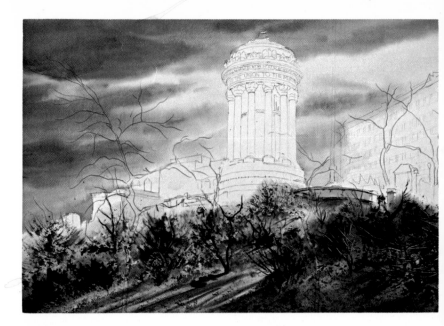

Step 6. *Until now, I've been working quickly to establish the values. Now I'll stop, leave the picture to dry thoroughly, and study it before my next attack.*

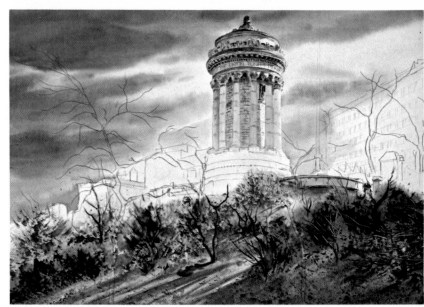

Step 7. *As I start back to work, I paint in the monument carefully with cadmium red, cobalt blue, and raw sienna, using the No. 2 and No. 6 brushes. I keep the warm and cool colors moving about and use light, airy washes to make the picture interesting. I add texture with a No. 2 brush and India ink.*

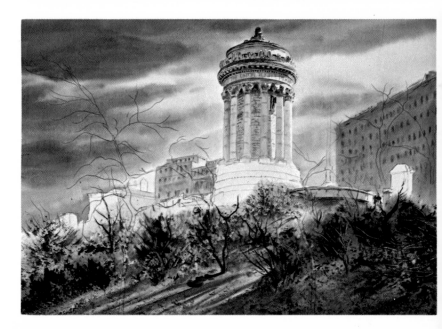

Step 8. *I re-wet the sky area with a soft 1" flat brush, just above the building on the right, and paint in cadmium red and cobalt blue mixed with raw umber to achieve a soft-edged effect. I suggest the windows with heavier mixtures of cobalt blue and raw umber and paint the building in back of the monument with cadmium red, cobalt blue, and a touch of raw umber.*

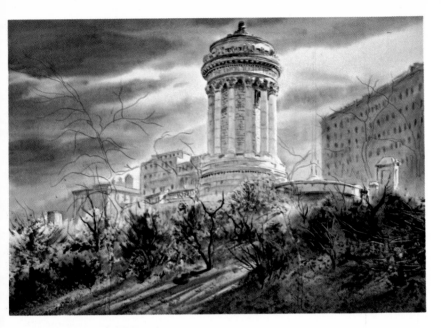

Step 9. *I paint in the rest of the buildings by applying washes of cadmium red, burnt sienna, raw umber, and ink directly to the dry paper. While some of these direct washes are still wet, I introduce India ink with a No. 2 brush. I re-wet the monument in sections, paint wet-in-wet with cadmium red, cobalt blue, and raw sienna, and texture lightly with burnt sienna and ink.*

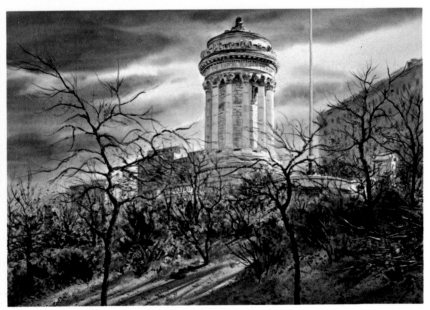

Step 10. *I paint in the trees with raw umber, burnt sienna, and ink, then fiddle around until I arrive at a pleasing arrangement of texture and pattern. I mask out the area around the flagpole with masking tape, quickly sponge the pole out of the sky area, carefully remove the tape, and paint the pole with a light purple wash.*

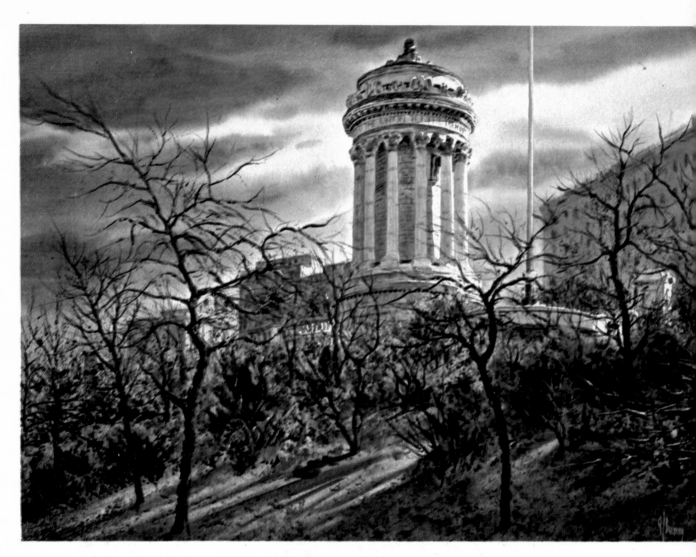

Soldiers' and Sailors' Monument. *To complete the painting, I gently lift a peak of light out of the bushes on the right with a small sponge and delicately tint the area with sap green. This gives better balance to the lighting. Finally, I paint the tree in the left foreground to halt the sweep of long shadows, and the picture seems complete.*

This old building was razed during a facelifting in Pittsburgh. What you see is the back of the building, which I found more interesting than the front. This painting is a study in off-center front lighting, and the unique, arched windows and protruding structures make it extremely desirable to paint. I'll use a sheet of 300 lb. cold-pressed Arches paper, the usual painting tools and palette, and one more color—alizarin crimson. I'll also use white tempera in the last step.

COURTHOUSE IN OFF-CENTER FRONT LIGHTING

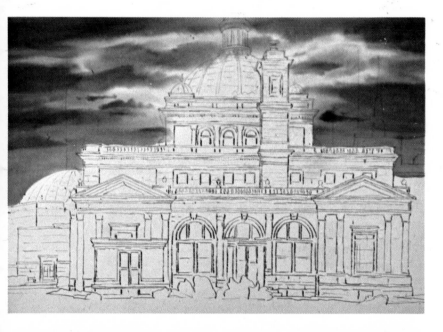

Step 1. *I double-wet the sky, cutting my strokes short around the lower part of the building, but running them over onto the main dome to allow for softer edges in this area. At this point, I flood in cadmium red and alizarin crimson in rather strong washes, then work in heavy washes of cobalt blue and burnt sienna for the cloud formations and leave the painting to dry.*

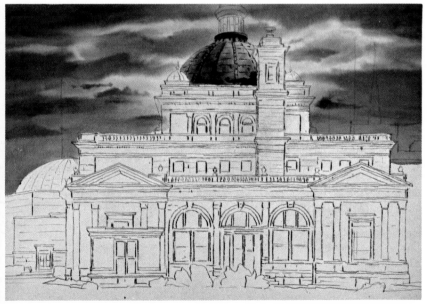

Step 2. *I work the main structure of the dome in values very close to those at the extreme edges of the sky to give an airy form to the dome. I add cobalt blue with a touch of sap green, brush in burnt sienna arbitrarily, and use a small brush loaded with black ink to describe the form.*

Step 3. *I paint in the top of the dome next, with warm and cool colors, and flood in touches of raw sienna and burnt sienna for the chimney. I mix a touch of cobalt blue into the chimney for a color change and use the ink technique for details. Then I paint in the small domes with cobalt blue, raw sienna, and ink.*

Step 4. *I wet the area under the dome with clear water and paint in raw sienna, cadmium red, and cobalt blue wet-in-wet, switching bits of color back and forth to create motion. I paint in the windows and decorative elements with darker mixtures of cobalt blue, burnt sienna, and ink.*

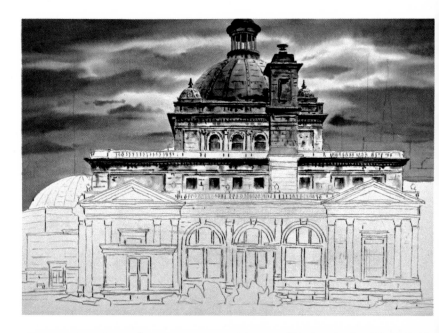

Step 5. *I continue the same procedure as I work down the monument, wetting the next area, introducing colors in warm and cool arrangements, and adding deeper values. I use black ink for the deepest shadows and for general definition.*

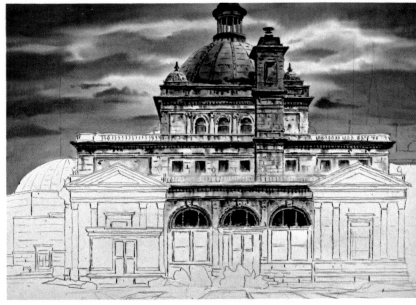

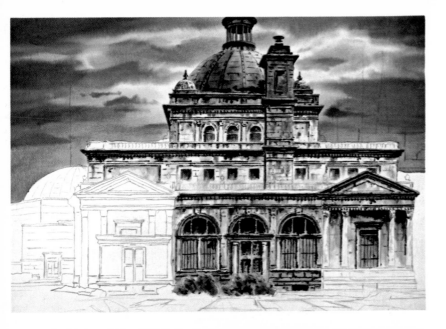

Step 6. *On I go—wetting and re-wetting new areas, feeding in a bit of complementary color, and bringing it together with deeper colors and black ink. For the bushes in the front foreground, I wet the area and add sap green, burnt sienna, cobalt blue, and ink.*

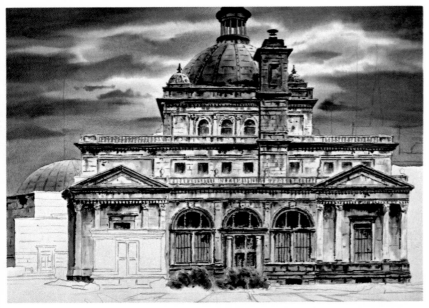

Step 7. *I wet the stones under the bottom windows and paint in cobalt blue, burnt sienna, ink, and a touch of cadmium red. I put in the dome on the other building with cobalt blue, sap green, and ink, and continue to work various sections of the buildings wet-in-wet with warm and cool vibrating colors.*

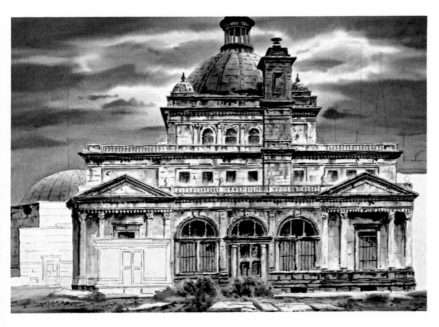

Step 8. *I double-wet the foreground and run in washes of burnt sienna, raw umber, and cobalt blue with a 1" flat brush. I introduce sap green and cobalt blue into the wet washes for small bits of growth, and spatter the whole foreground with darker color while it's still damp.*

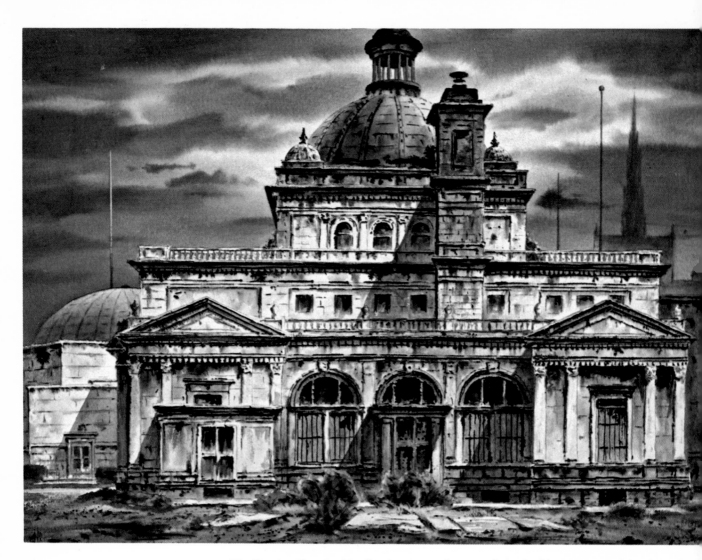

The Passing Parade. *Finally, I paint in the rest of the building areas and let them dry. Then I paint the cast shadows with cobalt blue and cadmium red, and warm them up with raw sienna, using a No. 10 round brush. I re-wet the sky in the right corner with a fixative blower and clear water, and I paint in the distant steeple with cobalt blue, burnt sienna, and a touch of cadmium red. Now I re-wet the left side of the sky, deepen it with cobalt blue, cadmium red, and burnt sienna, and indicate the flagpole and other vertical poles with dark color. I use burnt sienna and white tempera to put in the light pole on the dome in back.*

This is another study in off-center front lighting. The stained and pitted coral rocks and statuary make for an interesting picture; my philosophy is to keep it light and airy, reflecting the atmosphere of the tropics. This time, I'll use the same materials and tools, and my No. 10 red sable oil brush.

MANSION IN OFF-CENTER FRONT LIGHTING

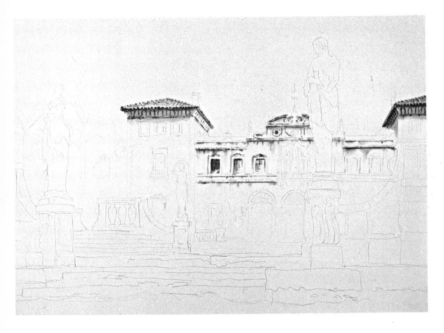

Step 1. *I tint the tile rooftops with cadmium red and a touch of burnt sienna and add detail in ink. Then I add raw sienna and cadmium red wet-in-wet on the front of the building and define it with ink and more color.*

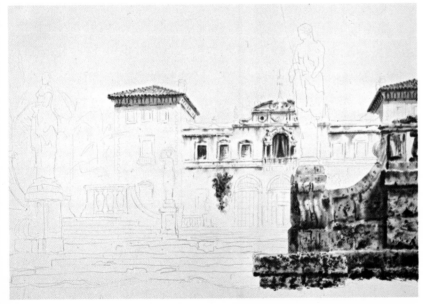

Step 2. *I indicate the growth in the front section of the building with some sap green and raw sienna and let this dry. Next, I wet the heavy stone structure on the barge in the right foreground and render it with cobalt blue, burnt sienna, raw sienna, and ink. I stipple it lightly with a sponge and a deep mixture of the same colors and ink.*

Step 3. *I wet the rest of the stone barge with clear water and use the same colors and techniques to complete it. On the steps, I paint the same colors, in short vertical strokes, with a flat No. 10 red sable oil brush. Then I wet the sky area with clear water and put in the foliage.*

Step 4. *I wet the bottom of the picture with a sponge and clear water, flood in cobalt blue and sap green for the water, and paint in washes of burnt sienna and cobalt blue with a No. 10 round brush.*

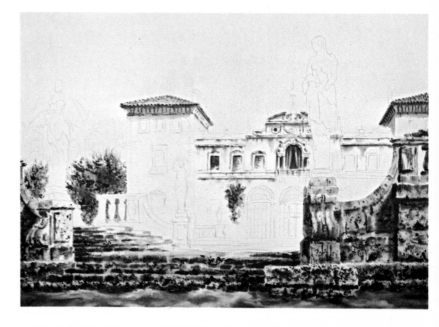

Step 5. *I wet the sky area with clear water and flood in cobalt blue with a touch of sap green as a basic sky value. To strengthen this area and attract the eye to the center of the composition, I add high clouds with burnt sienna and cobalt blue.*

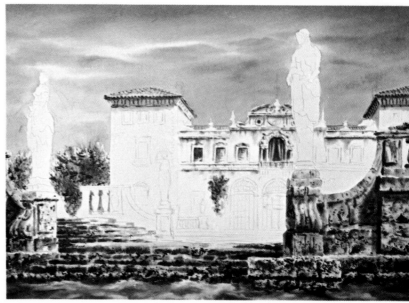

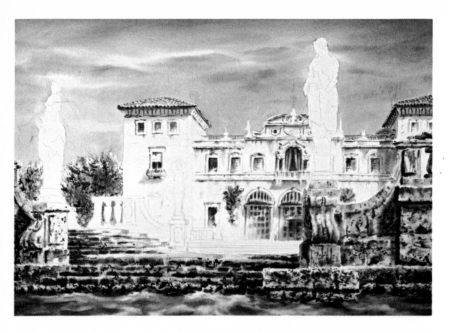

Step 6. *I re-wet the building front and paint the entrances wet-in-wet with cobalt blue and burnt sienna. I use cadmium yellow on the awnings and mix warm and cool grays for the door and the rest of the windows.*

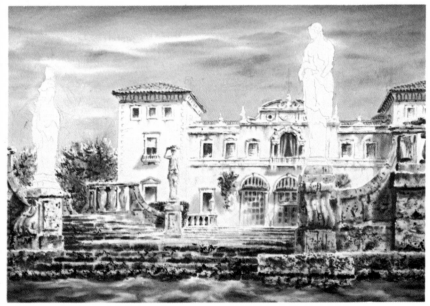

Step 7. *I add the statue and the balustrades on the stairway of the main building and on the barge. I wet these areas separately with clear water and work wet-in-wet with small brushes and cobalt blue, burnt sienna, raw sienna, and ink.*

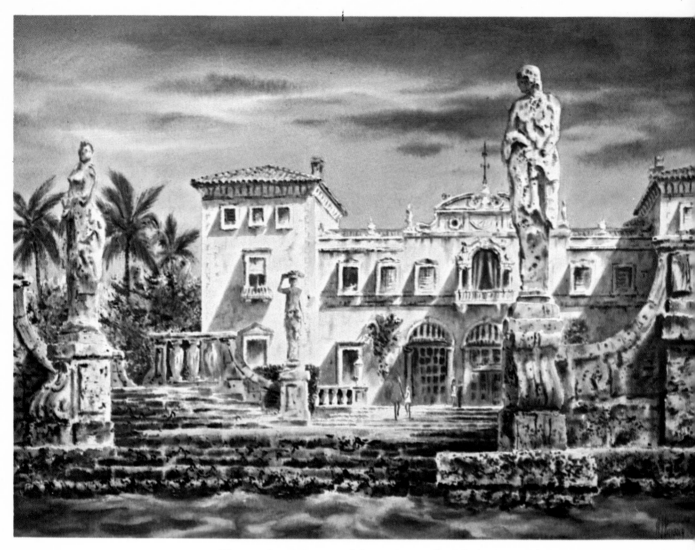

Vizcaya. *I wet the rest of the statues and work the same color scheme into them, along with sponged-in touches of ink to suggest pitted coral. I block out the top statue with masking tape (see page 129, "Altering Sky"), re-wet the sky, and blow pure water on it with a fixative blower. Then I quickly paint in the darker clouds and add some palm trees in the lower left sky. For the final step, I add the figures.*

This old mission, with crumbling walls against a backlit sky, is an interesting study in subtle silhouettes. The low-key greens and the rust earth colors are always interesting to paint in the shadows of late day. Again, I'll soak and stretch a sheet of Arches 300 lb. cold-pressed paper. My palette and the tools will be the same as in previous demonstrations.

MEXICAN MISSION IN BACK LIGHTING

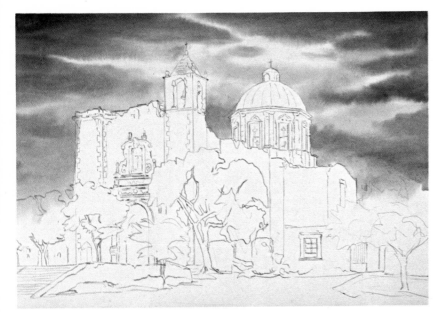

Step 1. *I double-wet the entire area behind the building and flood in raw sienna. Then I paint in washes of cobalt blue and burnt sienna, with touches of permanent blue for the darker clouds, using a 1" flat brush.*

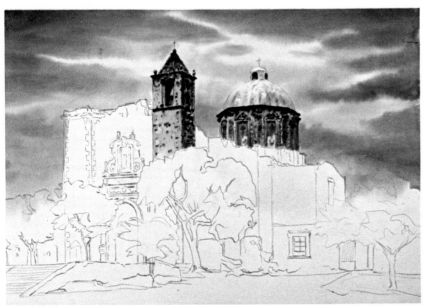

Step 2. *I paint the dome in cadmium red and burnt sienna, and the tile on the bell tower roof in cadmium red and cobalt blue. I use cadmium red, cobalt blue, and raw sienna on the walls of both structures, with cadmium red and burnt sienna for the decorative bricks. I use a treatment of ink throughout, to indicate detail and wash in the windows below the dome.*

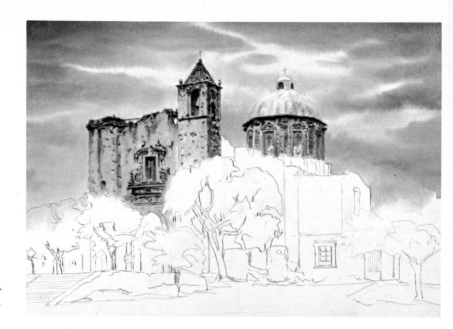

Step 3. *I use the same colors and treatment to complete the front façade, then draw in detail with inklines.*

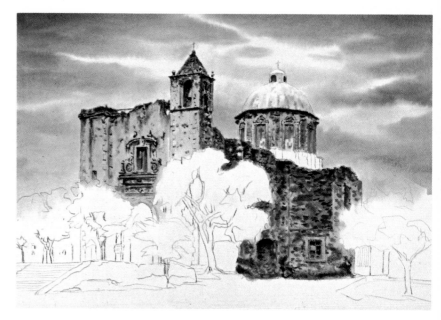

Step 4. *To describe the crumbling walls, I first wet the entire area, then work in burnt sienna, permanent blue, and cobalt blue wet-in-wet. I texture with a brush and ink. For the brick trim around the window, I use cadmium red with burnt sienna and a touch of cobalt blue.*

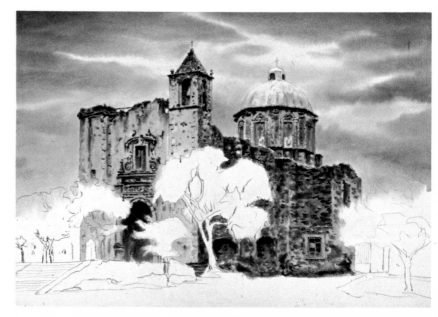

Step 5. *I pre-wet the rest of the area and continue working the same way with the same colors, varying the values slightly to keep the different areas alive.*

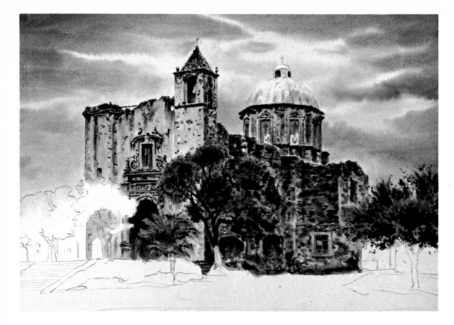

Step 6. *I re-wet the tree areas with the flat brush and clear water and paint in the base colors—raw sienna and sap green—with the No. 6 brush. I follow this up with the sponge treatment, using raw sienna, sap green, cobalt blue, and black India ink. Then I drag a small No. 2 brush loaded with ink through the tree on the right, to create a different effect, and paint in the small tree in front with sap green, raw sienna, and ink.*

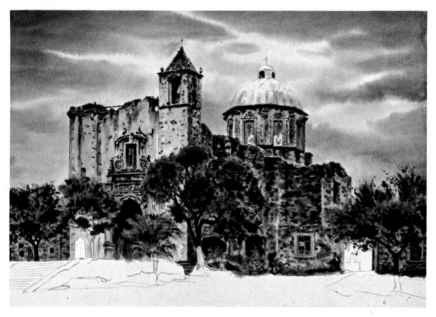

Step 7. *On the left side, I paint the wall and trees, using the treatment I used in Steps 3 and 5. I paint in the wall and foliage wet, the trunk and branches dry. Then I add the far right wall and texture it, using burnt sienna and cobalt blue with ink.*

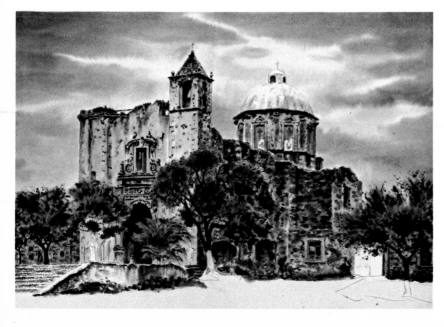

Step 8. *I work the main stairs and the crumbling wall around them wet-in-wet, using cadmium red, raw sienna, cobalt blue, and ink. For the growth along the bottom of the wall, I use sap green with black ink.*

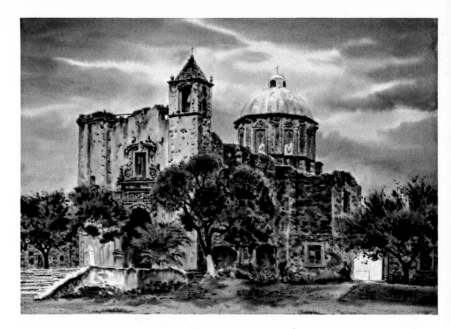

Step 9. *I wet the foreground with the flat brush; when it's almost dry, I use a fanned-out brush to apply raw sienna and raw umber, with touches of burnt sienna and sap green. I also use some drybrush here.*

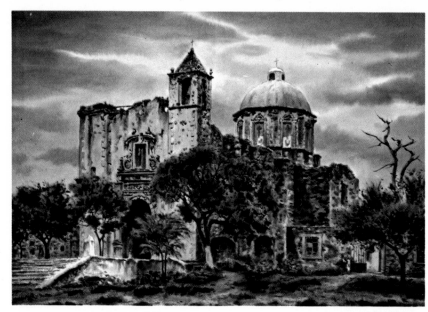

Step 10. *The foreground, though decent, is too bland; so I rewet it with the flat brush and work back into it with bold strokes of the same colors, to give it more strength. I also inject a tree into the sky at the lower right, to help balance the composition.*

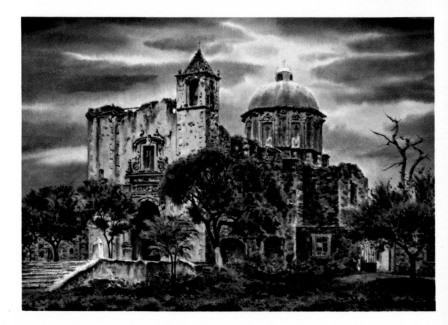

Step 11. *The foreground, though still acceptable, seems to "jump out" too much. So I sponge it out completely with clear water and repaint it with the same colors in a lower key.*

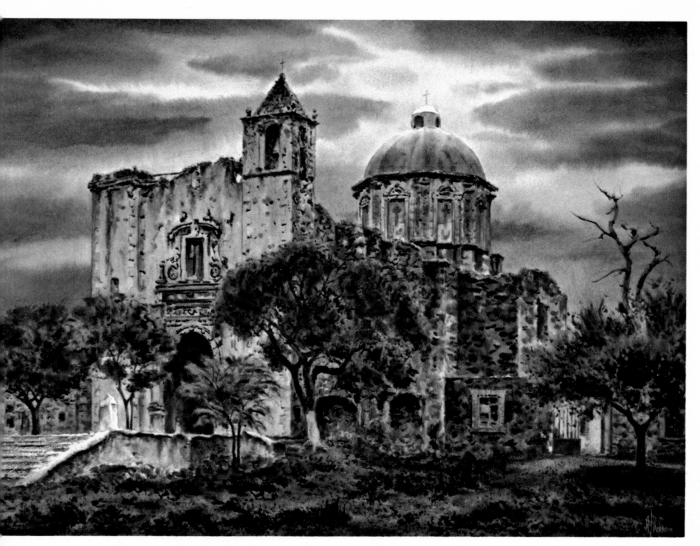

Mexican Mission. *Now the sky seems weak, so I'll try the impossible! I mask out the buildings with tape and re-wet the sky by blowing water on it. I drop deep washes of pure raw sienna off the brush into the wet lower sky and tilt the board around until the washes are fairly even. Then I paint in burnt sienna, cobalt blue, and permanent blue boldly and quickly with the flat brush. Here, I'll quit and hope for the best. You can compare the results with the picture in Step 10. I hope you'll see the improvement!*

DEMONSTRATION 26

MEXICAN MISSION IN FRONT LIGHTING

When I finish a painting, I sometimes think it would be interesting to do the same subject in an entirely different light. So, I'll paint the composition again and take the liberty of moving the bell tower to the other side of the dome to create a better grouping and more structural interest. This time I'll paint a sunlit version. I'll use the same tools, paper, and palette.

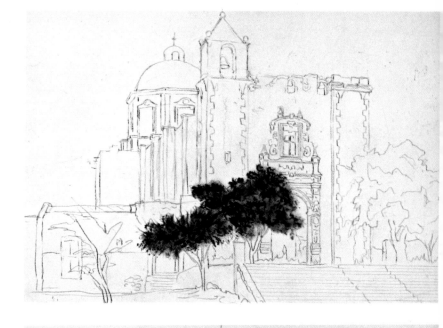

Step 1. *First, I wet the center area with clear water and loosely paint in the trees with a No. 10 brush and a mixture of sap green and raw sienna. Then I scoop up pure cobalt blue, sap green, and raw umber on a sponge, stipple the colors into the wet wash, pick up a little ink on the sponge, and lightly stipple it on top of the other moist colors.*

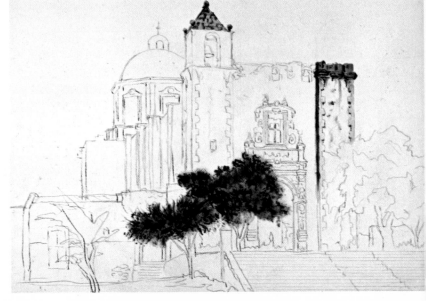

Step 2. *The tile roof is next. On the dry paper, I paint cadmium red, with the slightest touch of cadmium orange, and texture it with ink while it's still moist. Now for the right section of the building. I use burnt sienna and cobalt blue at the top, and cadmium red as a light tint for the decorative brickwork. I put the subtle stains and textures in wet on the front of the building.*

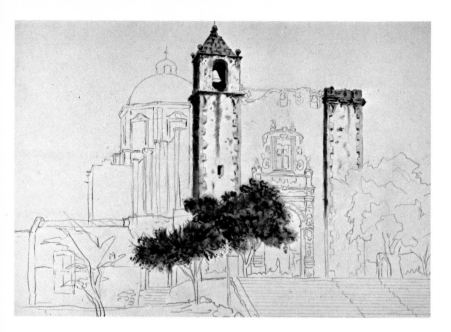

Step 3. *I paint the rest of the bell tower by wetting the area and working in the same manner. Instead of raw sienna, I use raw umber generously to warm up the shadows. (I've run short of raw sienna, but you can see that you don't have to be stuck on one color—you can get along with a close substitute.)*

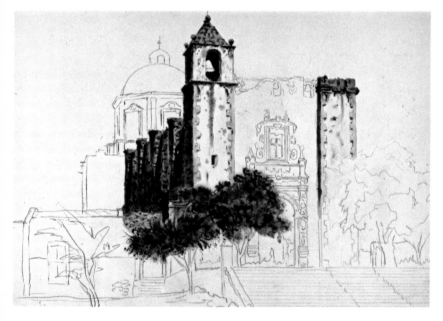

Step 4. *I wet the walls and buttresses on the left with water and work wet-in-wet, using cobalt blue and burnt sienna on a No. 6 brush. I texture it with a No. 2 brush and black ink.*

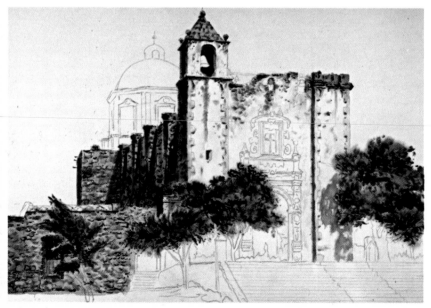

Step 5. *Again, I wet the remaining areas on the left with clear water and fill them in as I did in Step 4. Notice that the warm and cool underwashes of burnt sienna and cobalt blue give life to the areas. To depict the stone-work, I use a No. 2 brush and ink. I use a brush, a sponge, and the colors used in Step 1, to work in the tree in front of this wall. I wet the area for the tree at the right, insert that tree with the same procedure and colors, complete the lower part of the wall behind it, and the shadow of the tree with a No. 2 brush and ink.*

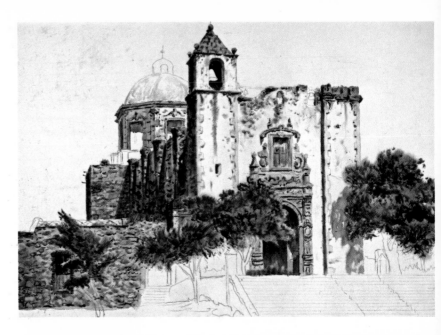

Step 6. *I suggest the top of the dome by washing in a pre-tint of cadmium red and burnt sienna, the lower portion by adding cobalt blue and raw umber mixed with ink. Now I re-wet the front of the building and paint the façade with light washes of cadmium red and burnt sienna, strengthened with cobalt blue and burnt sienna mixed with ink. In the doorway, I paint a deep mixture of cobalt blue, cadmium red, and ink.*

Step 7. *I wet the entire sky area with water and paint in cobalt blue with a touch of ultramarine blue and sap green. Then I add the cloud design, using cobalt blue and burnt sienna in warm gray washes.*

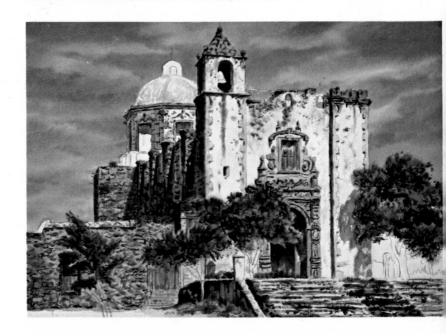

Step 8. *With the same colors I used on the building and shrubbery, I paint the main steps, the small supporting wall, and the growth around them wet-in-wet. I paint the steps and the small entrance on the left with cadmium red and cadmium orange, adding touches of gray that I pick up from my palette.*

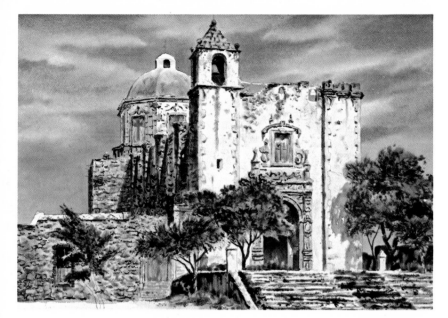

Step 9. *Never satisfied, I now sponge out the lower left portion of the sky over the wall and paint in heavy amounts of cobalt blue with a touch of ultramarine blue and sap green. To soften the sting of these pure colors, I use a trace of burnt sienna. When this is dry, I take a chance and mask out the dome and the tower with masking tape, re-wet the area above by spraying it with clear water, and deepen the blues with ultramarine and cobalt blue. When this area is dry, I deepen the color of the dome with cadmium red, burnt sienna, and cobalt blue.*

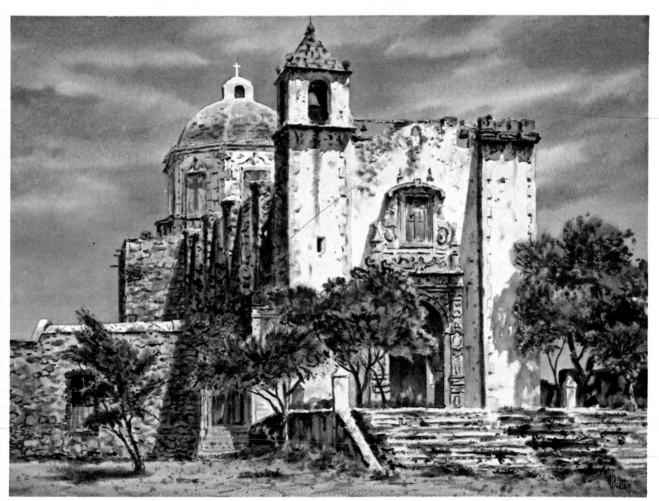

Against All Time. *Luckily, I've found half a tube of raw sienna deep down in my paint-box, so I re-wet the foreground and paint this color in wet with a touch of burnt sienna and raw umber. I paint in spots of small green shrubs with the usual greens and stipple them with ink. When the foreground is dry, I spatter it with darker colors and use some drybrush. The cast shadows on the front of the building are next, and I paint them with cobalt blue and cadmium red, warmed with raw umber. On the stone wall, I use cadmium red and cobalt blue, warmed up with a touch of burnt sienna. Finally, to create better contrast and more texture, I alter the dome again: re-wet the area gently with clear water, and apply deeper values of the same colors, strengthened with ink.*

DEMONSTRATION 27

COMPOSITE PAINTING, USING VARIED TECHNIQUES

The purpose of this demonstration is to explore the techniques you can use in a picture of several buildings. I'll show you how to blend a section of one building into a portion of another building. My materials will be the same: a sheet of Arches 300 lb. watercolor paper, prepared by stretching; the usual palette; the same tools.

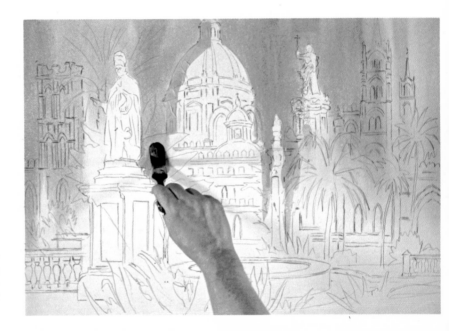

Step 1. *I wet the sky area with clear water and let the water run onto some of the buildings. Then I flood in washes of raw sienna and touches of burnt sienna with a flat 1" brush.*

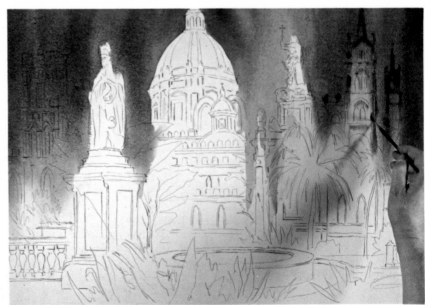

Step 2. *I mix heavy washes of cobalt blue, permanent blue, and burnt sienna, keeping them on the cool side, and paint them in with vertical strokes. Now I render some of the buildings with a No. 6 and a No. 2 brush, using thick mixtures of color and ink.*

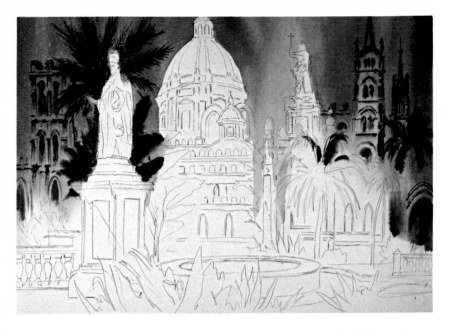

Step 3. *While the main washes are still damp and workable, I continue drawing and detailing the buildings with thick mixtures of permanent blue and burnt sienna. I hurriedly paint and sponge the palm and cypress trees into place with burnt sienna, cobalt blue, raw sienna, and ink. Then I let these areas dry.*

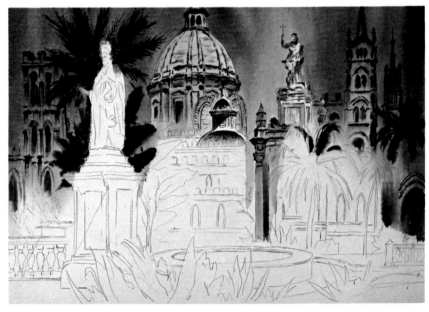

Step 4. *I wet the center dome and wash in pale tints of cadmium red, raw sienna, and cobalt blue. Then with the same colors, I paint the statuary and the smaller dome in dry.*

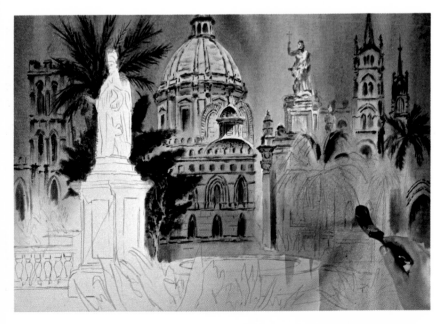

Step 5. *I continue to wet different areas and work in warm and cool mixtures of cobalt blue, permanent blue, and raw sienna. I inject trees wet-in-wet and stipple them.*

COMPOSITE PAINTING, USING VARIED TECHNIQUES 117

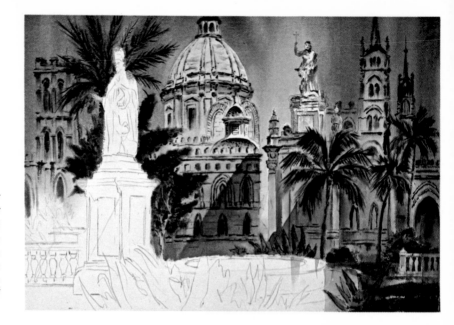

Step 6. *I paint in the area in back of the balustrade with deep mixtures of cobalt blue, burnt sienna, and ink and add cadmium red wet-in-wet for the flowers. For grass, I paint and stipple in sap green and raw sienna, with a touch of black ink. After the first washes dry, I add cast shadows of cobalt blue and cadmium red.*

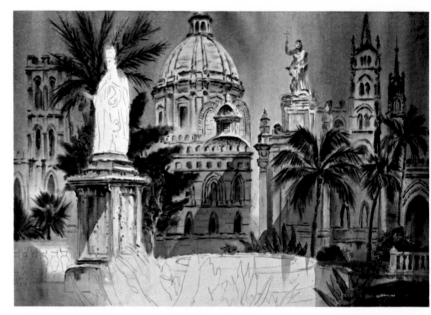

Step 7. *I continue re-wetting and painting, injecting burnt sienna into the greenery to warm up the colors in those areas. I paint the base of the large statue wet-in-wet with cadmium red cobalt blue, and raw sienna, and spatter it with ink. When the washes are dry, I add the cast shadow, using cobalt blue, cadmium red, and raw sienna.*

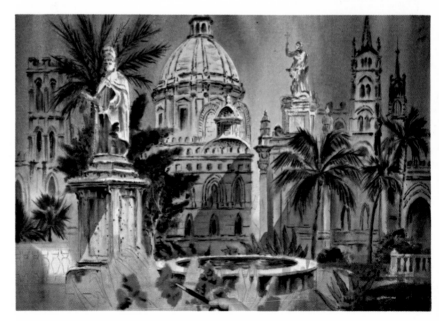

Step 8. *I double-wet the foreground in front of the fountain and brush in a cool gray mixture of cobalt blue, cadmium red, and burnt sienna. I use cadmium red for the flowers, and texture the area with black ink.*

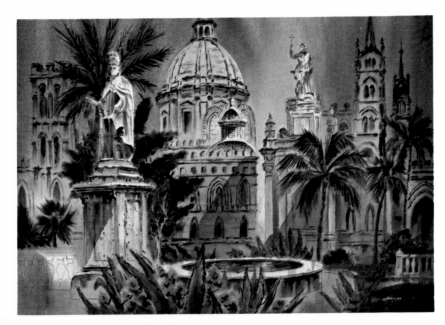

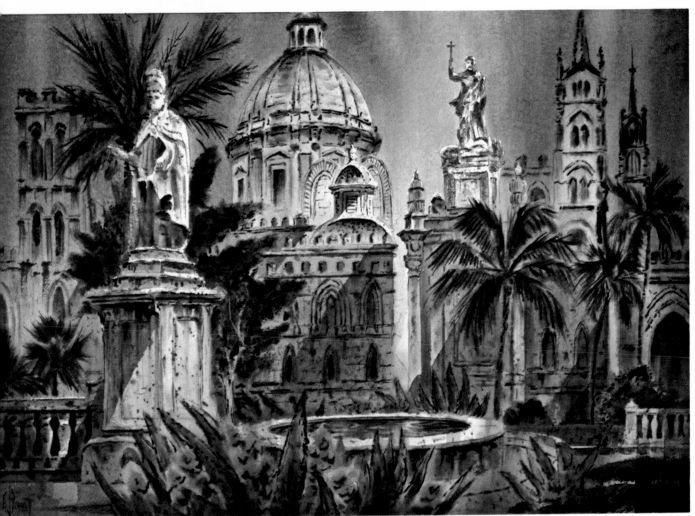

Step 9. *For the leaves, I use sap green, with touches of cobalt blue and permanent blue, and warm them up with raw umber and raw sienna. I texture these with black ink and the No. 2 brush.*

Palermo. *Finally, I paint in the balustrade on the left, then alter and enlarge some cast shadows on the right. With color and ink, I deepen the large dome to help improve the composition and further integrate the values.*

DEMONSTRATION 28

CASTLE ST. ANGELO IN DRAMATIC LIGHTING

The stonework and the structure of the bridge and castle of this famous Roman landmark are magnificent—pitted, stained, and crumbling—and the shadows and the dramatic sky add excitement to the subject. I'm going to paint this in small sections, so I can discuss the details as I go along. I'll use the usual materials and tools, along with a bleach, such as Clorox, and some white vinegar.

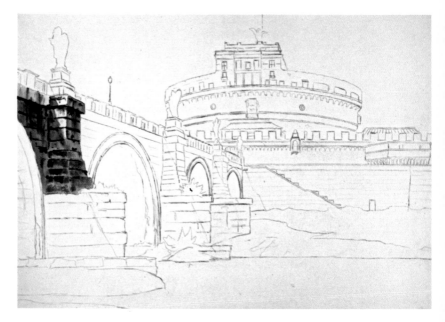

Step 1. *First, I wet a small area of the bridge with clear water and wash in a pale tint of raw sienna. I work in burnt sienna and cobalt blue next to each other to define the cast shadow and to create a vibration of warm color against cool color. Then I indicate the stone texture with black ink and a No. 2 brush.*

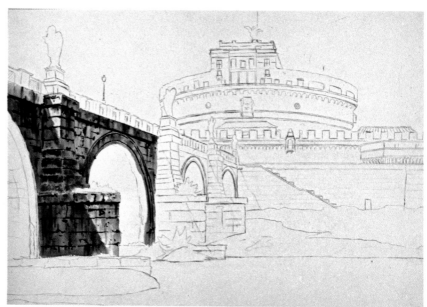

Step 2. *I continue the same procedure, wetting the next small area of the bridge and painting in raw sienna first, then burnt sienna and cobalt blue for color and shadow, and finally using the black ink treatment.*

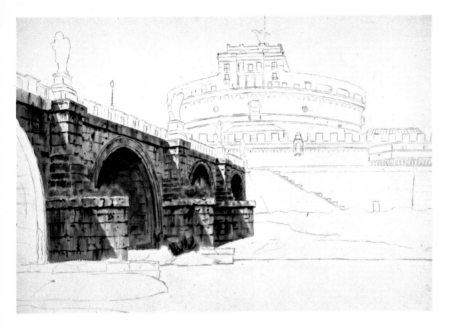

Step 3. *I complete the bridge by wetting and re-wetting small areas and introducing color and ink. I introduce a pale tint of raw sienna into all but the closest archway. Then I work a thick mixture of cadmium red, burnt sienna, and cobalt blue in wet, to darken the shadows of the arches under the bridge.*

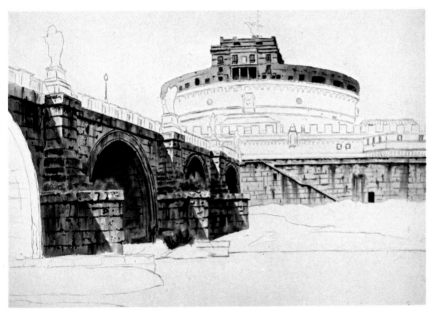

Step 4. *I wet the stone retaining wall on the far side of the river with clear water and gently float in pale tints of raw sienna and cobalt blue, painting them next to each other in a random arrangement. I brush burnt sienna into this wet area to create stains, and I use black ink carefully and ever so lightly to interpret the brickwork. Then I wet the top of the tower and use the same warm and cool colors, in the same manner that I used them on the bridge.*

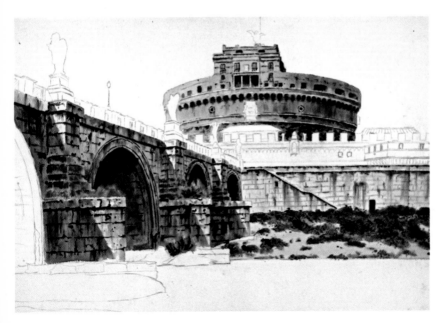

Step 5. *I handle the rest of the tower with the same colors and techniques. I wet the far river bank, and paint in a basewash of raw sienna and cadmium red. I sponge in raw sienna, sap green, and touches of burnt sienna for the growth and stipple it lightly with a sponge and ink.*

Step 6. *I paint the rest of the buttresses and towers by wetting them and alternately washing in burnt sienna, cobalt blue, and cadmium red; I define these areas with black ink. I paint the footings of the bridge with the colors and procedure I used in Step 1. I add the growth at the base of the footings by painting in deep mixtures of sap green, burnt sienna, raw sienna, and cobalt blue, and work into them with a brush and ink to establish even darker values.*

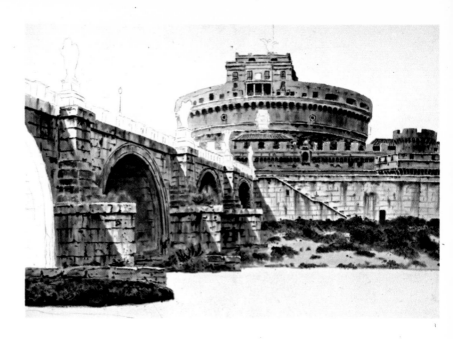

Step 7. *The way I've drawn the first arch seems wrong, so I'll correct it. First, I re-wet the small bridge area around the arch and patch it up with the same colors. Next, I wet the arch and paint it in, with the colors I used in Step 3. Then I wet the paper in the foreground and wash in cobalt blue and burnt sienna, as a start in establishing the water, and indicate the reflections of the growth on the far bank.*

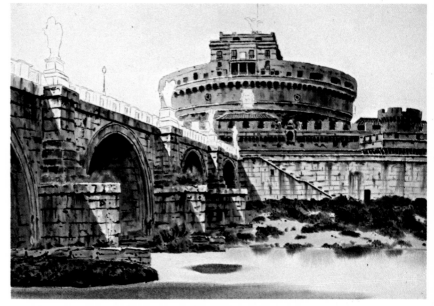

Step 8. *I continue to paint the water with a No. 10 round brush, using only cobalt blue and burnt sienna, then let it dry. For the growth in the lower left corner, I sponge in some raw sienna, sap green, and burnt sienna.*

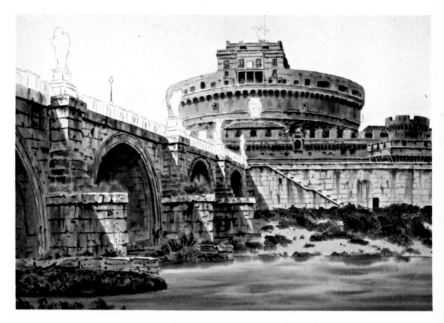

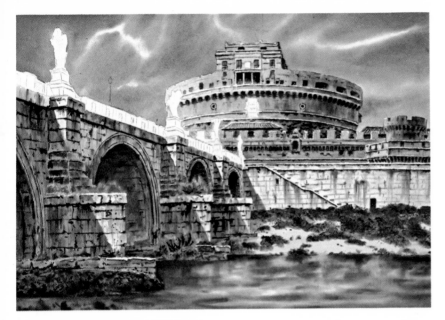

Step 9. *At this stage, the water and growth don't really appeal to me. They seem too "hard" and they don't blend well with the rest of the painting. So I sponge out the entire foreground and use the same colors and procedure to paint it back in, making an attempt to show more reflections. I paint the growth of grass and weeds, along with the water, wet-in-wet. The effect seems a little better now.*

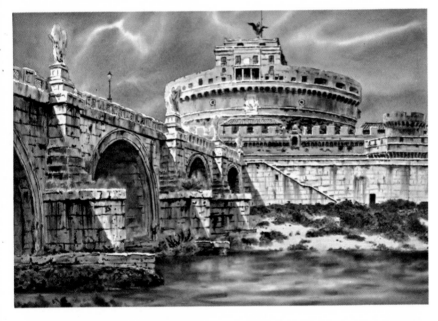

Step 10. *I paint in the top of the bridge, the statuary, and the lamp, using cobalt blue and burnt sienna with ink. I very carefully re-wet a small area of the sky over the castle and paint in the figure of St. Michael with a small brush and a thick mixture of almost-dry burnt sienna and cobalt blue.*

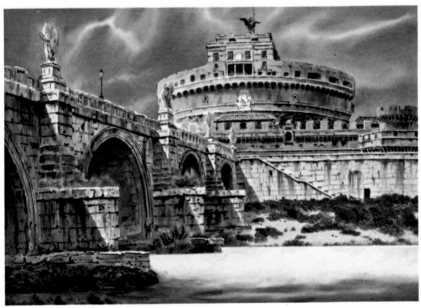

Step 11. *The water still bothers me: it still doesn't look right, so I'll try again. I carefully block out the bridge and the river bank with masking tape and sponge out the center. Then I gently flood in some diluted Clorox on a brush to bleach out the sap green, and I neutralize it with white vinegar. I do not recommend this procedure, by the way; it weakens and discolors the paper. Fortunately, my paper still seems sturdy in this area, with no discoloration.*

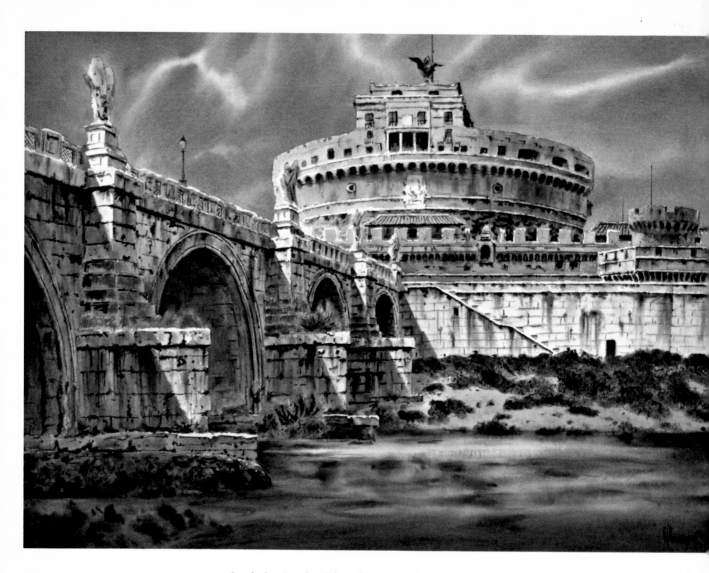

Castle St. Angelo. *When this area is bone dry, I re-wet it using a fixative blower, and paint it again with the same colors and techniques, making the small changes you can see if you compare this picture with Step 9. On impulse, I gently brush in some pale tints of alizarin crimson to complement the existing colors in the water. I also alter the parapet on the right around the small tower, letting the colors run right out of the picture, instead of crowding the structure into that corner. Finally, I paint a flagpole on the tower with burnt sienna and ink to establish another vertical line.*

In this demonstration, I'll show you all the busy things that I love to do. I'll use a double, elephant-size sheet of Arches watercolor paper, cut to 36" x 25" and stretched on a large 3/4" plywood board; the usual tools and materials; and some crumpled paper for stippling. Now for the fun of painting this!

RUINS, USING VARIED TECHNIQUES

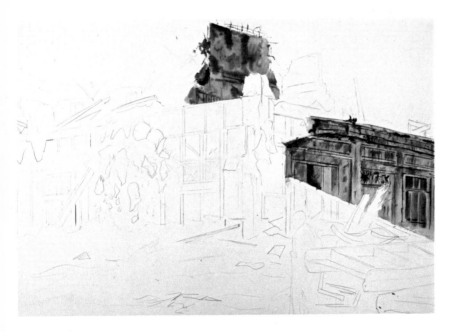

Step 1. *I wet the top area of the ruins with clear water and paint in a base-wash of cadmium red, permanent blue, and cobalt blue. Then I introduce raw sienna into the wet color with a No. 6 round brush and render the plaster cracks with ink. I paint the lower section in a similar manner, but here, I keep the bluish-purple color dominant.*

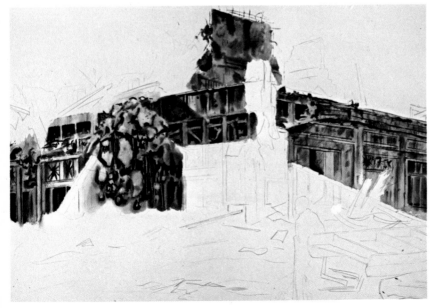

Step 2. *I wet the left side and paint in the falling, crumbly plaster with a tint of raw sienna, cobalt blue, and cadmium red. Then I use thick mixtures of the same colors and ink for definition. With a small round brush handle, I squeeze out the suggestion of the metal lath and the plaster hanging from it. I re-wet this area and the rest of the structure and paint in cobalt blue, burnt sienna, raw sienna, and permanent blue, working detail into the wet washes with pure ink.*

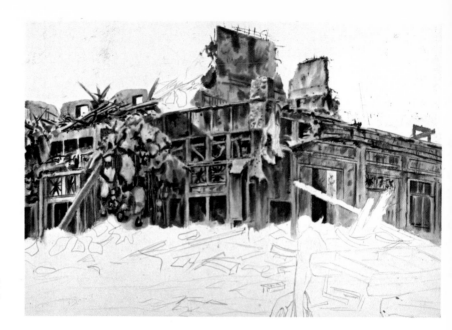

Step 3. *I attack the center section next, using the same procedures, colors, and ink. I paint around the fallen rafter first, then I paint it in.*

Step 4. *I wet the entire foreground, except the boy, with clear water and wash in permanent blue, cobalt blue, and burnt sienna as an underwash for the large area of rubble. I flood in raw sienna and burnt sienna for a warm, middle, sunlit tone, and again I use permanent blue, cobalt blue, and burnt sienna for the foreground shadow. To suggest rubble at the base of the building, I crumple up newspaper and scoop up a mixture of burnt sienna, permanent blue, and ink and stamp it into the damp wash. While this is wet, I scrape it with a brush handle and scatter ink strokes around it with a small brush, to simulate broken pipes, boards, metal, etc. Then I throw brushstrokes of burnt sienna and black ink into the foreground with a No. 6 round brush, to help create the feeling of scattered rubble.*

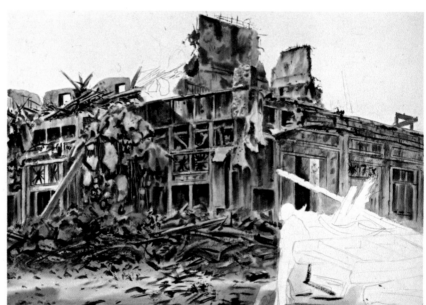

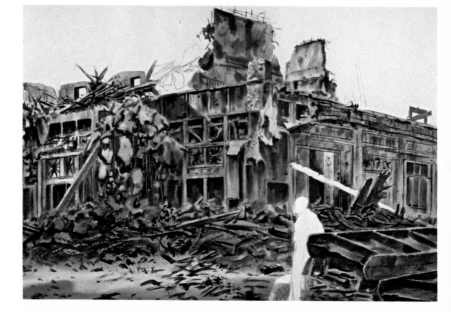

Step 5. *I now wet the area in back of the figure and paint it in, using the same colors and techniques I used in Step 4. I work the steel girder by wetting it separately and adding burnt sienna, raw sienna, and permanent blue wet-in-wet, with a touch of an ink-line here and there for definition.*

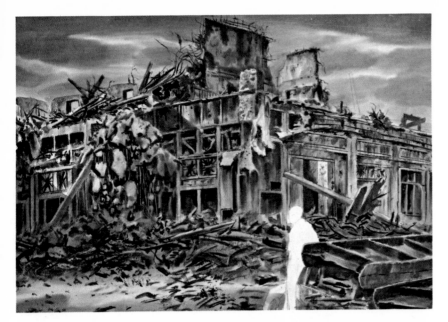

Step 6. *Now, I wet the sky and put in small areas of cobalt blue with a 1" flat brush, to indicate patches of blue sky. I mix permanent blue and cobalt blue with burnt sienna and boldly paint them in with the 1" flat brush, using large, sweeping strokes. I render the clouds in a deeper value than the blue sky and let the area dry. Then I place a piece of cardboard over the upper left side of the picture, spray the lower left area of the building with water, and drop a deep mixture of permanent blue, cobalt blue, and burnt sienna onto it in large quantities, from the tip of the No. 10 round brush. Next, I pick up the board and tilt it around until the pigment is distributed in a pleasing shadow wash and let it dry.*

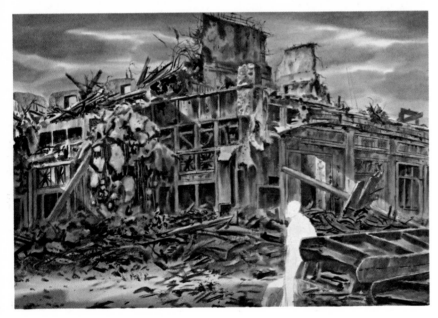

Step 7. *I use the same procedure for the shadow on the upper right side of the building, this time masking the lower right side of the building with cardboard first. I make the value deep for this shadow, so it will be dark enough when it dries over the colors beneath. When the shadow wash is almost dry, I strengthen some of the existing forms with a brush, color, and ink.*

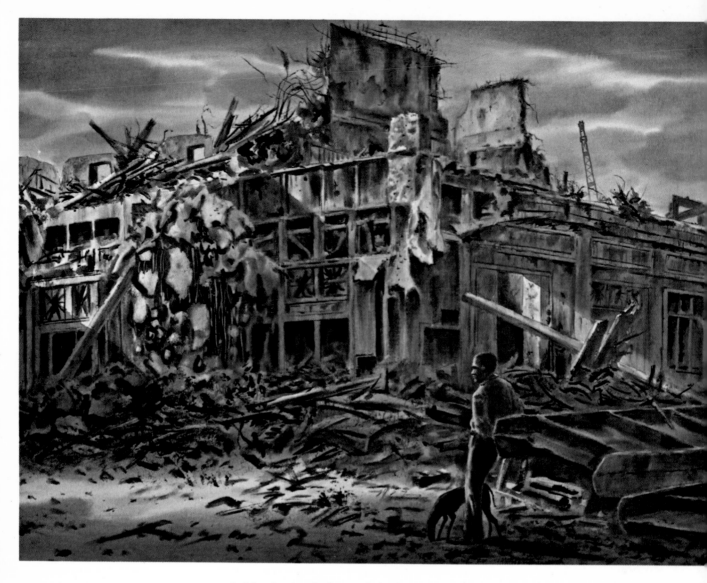

Jericho. *I paint the boy and the dog in last. I use raw sienna for the boy's shirt; cadmium red and cobalt blue for shadowing on the shirt; raw sienna for the pants; burnt sienna, cobalt blue, and ink for shadows on the pants; and burnt sienna and cadmium red for his face. I use burnt sienna and black ink for the dog and scatter around a few more textures in the foreground to complete the picture.*

PROBLEMS AND HOW TO CORRECT THEM

There are many reasons for correcting a particular area of a painting: it may not look as you had originally intended; it may seem to "jar" with the rest of the composition; it may be too dark or too light, too crowded or too sprawling, too warm or too cool. In this section, I'll show you the techniques—and the tricks—I use to correct areas of paintings that don't please me the first time. I've developed some of these techniques myself, and I use them at various stages of painting—from early to finished—as I see problem arising.

Altering Sky

Here are several steps you can take to salvage your painting when the sky is either too light or too dark and throws other values out of balance. Some of these techniques are quite simple, while some require great care to complete without disturbing other areas of the picture. The technique you use at any given time will depend on the nature of the problem and the composition of the painting involved.

The easiest way to alter a sky is to sponge it out *before* the original washes are dry. Try to decide immediately whether or not your sky area will be suitable (remember that washes dry lighter). If you don't think it will be acceptable, sponge it out *right away:* at least you'll remove all the pigment, without doing much damage to the paper underneath.

Although it's possible to sponge out sky areas *after* they've dried, it's a very difficult maneuver to pull off successfully; I strongly suggest that you *first* consider the following alternatives.

When the sky is too dark, study the painting to see if you can strengthen some other passages. More surrounding darks, for example, can make the sky area *seem* lighter by comparison. Sometimes, if the design of the picture permits it, you can simply trim off some of the sky area to weaken its influence on the rest of the composition.

If the sky is a simple, deep wash—and not too large an area—I sometimes lift out some of the pigment by

blotting it. I wet the area quickly with a large 1″ flat brush (never stroking in the same place twice), spread a paper towel over the wet area, and rub it gently with the heel of my hand. If a few light streaks and blotches are left in the sky area, I mix up a wash with the correct color and value, put my nose a few inches from the paper, and gently stipple the areas in with a No. 1 round brush. This procedure is not as difficult as it sounds: I've used it to repair many scrapes and damages that have occurred in the course of painting or handling.

Finally, if you must sponge out a sky that's already dry, be sure to first mask out the other important areas of the picture carefully with drafting tape and pieces of cardboard, then sponge out the sky with a clean sponge and clear water. When the area you're sponging out is almost white, gently add your new sky wash and hope for the best! When your wash dries, remove the tape very carefully. (It's impossible to use this masking technique on certain makes of paper: the surface of some papers lifts right off with the tape.)

There are a number of ways to *darken* a sky that's too light in value. If the sky is a simple, flat tone, just mix up a deep wash on your palette (*don't* mix it on the paper, or you'll disturb the original sky wash); then, with a flat brush, run the deeper wash quickly over the original sky and let it dry.

When you want to darken areas of sky at the *edges* of a painting, you can try this method. First, cover all the areas you want to protect by laying cardboard or heavy paper over them. Then, using a fixative blower, blow clear water on the exposed areas. (You can also use an atomizer, spray bomb, or spray can for this step.) Gently remove the masks and tilt the board to let the excess water run off the edges. Now, mix your new colors, drop them into the wet areas, and tilt the board again to let the new colors spread through the wet areas. I also use this method for central areas of sky, carefully controlling the amount of water I add. When I tilt the board around, I try to confine the water to the center, rather than let it run off.

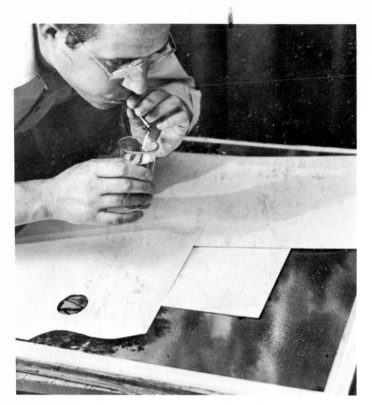

To darken an area of sky at the edge of a painting, cover the areas you want to protect with pieces of cardboard, then blow water on the sky area with a fixative blower. Add your darker colors and tilt the board around until the colors spread through the wet areas.

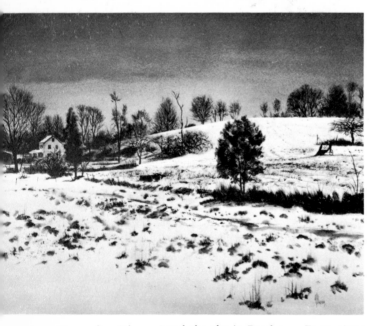

Even after I'd repainted the sky in Preakness Farm *three times, I decided that it still wasn't dark enough. So I blew water on the sky area with a fixative blower, waited until it was just damp, and used the blower to blow a soupy mixture of color along the top and outer edges. As it dried, the pigment blended smoothly into the underwash.*

I sometimes complete this operation in two stages: re-wetting and altering one area, then letting that dry while I re-wet and alter another area. As I said, every maneuver of this sort is dangerous and can sometimes result in the loss of a picture—and I always hope for the best when I make these corrections! In Step 9 of Demonstration 23, when I altered the sky, I was very lucky that the procedure worked out so well!

In the illustration of *Preakness Farm,* you can see the results of another method I use to darken sky areas. The sky was the first area of the painting I completed, and it gave me trouble right from the start. I sponged it out three times while it was still wet and repainted it. I let the third attempt dry, but by this time the paper had been so soaked with water that the values paled out as they dried. (Remember that watercolor always looks darker when it's wet and becomes lighter as it dries.)

I went on to complete the rest of the painting, but the sky still didn't have the strength and impact I wanted. So I used the fixative blower to re-wet the entire sky. Then I mixed burnt sienna and cobalt blue to the consistency of pea soup in a small glass while I let the water settle into the paper. When the area was just damp, I blew the soupy paint mixture along the top and outer edges of sky with a fixative blower. The small particles of pigment hit the paper in a spatter effect, then softened and blended into the underwash to create a smooth transition of values. Using the fixative blower this way gave me better control of the paint; a brush would have lifted off the underwash and left uneven streaks of color.

Now, let's suppose you decide to darken a sky by running some dark storm clouds across it. If the sky has a simple horizon line, you can mask it off with tape at the horizon line and cover the rest of the painting below the horizon with cardboard. Then tilt the board slightly, pour a jar of clean water over it, level the board, and let the water settle a bit. On your palette, mix up a substantial amount of your new value and drop some of it off the end of a brush into the various areas of sky to be darkened. Pick up the board and tilt it again until the colors flow and blend the way you want them to. Finally, level the board and let the washes dry.

I used a combination of some of these techniques to add dark clouds to the sky of *Vizcaya* in Step 8 of Demonstration 24. I put strips of regular masking tape over the upper part of the statue, extending them into the sky area. (The shape of the statue was still visible through the single layer of tape.) Then, I used an X-Acto knife blade to cut through the tape along the outline of the statue and removed the tape outside of this line by carefully peeling it away.

With a fixative blower, I carefully re-wet the entire sky area and tilted the board to let the excess water run off. Using a 1″ flat brush loaded with color, I carefully painted in the darker clouds. I used bold strokes, but was careful not to drag the brush through the same area twice, for fear of lifting out or streaking the original washes. When the area dried, I removed the tape and the sky seemed to have a smooth-

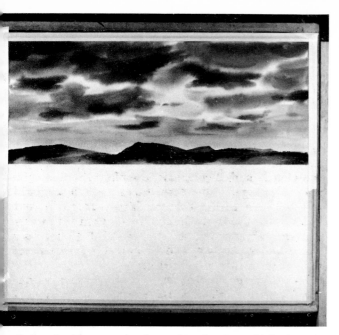

Before I add storm clouds to this sky, I mask the horizon line with tape and cover the section below with cardboard.

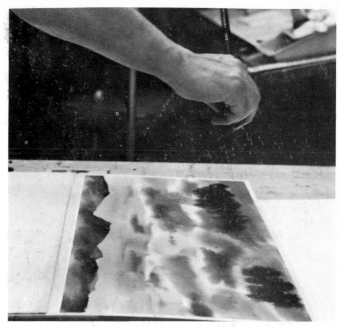

After I pour a jar of clean water over the sky area, I mix up a deep value on my palette and drop it onto the sky while it's still wet.

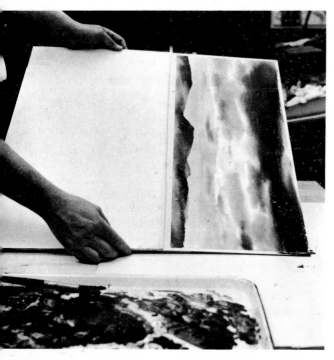

While the sky area and the new colors are still wet, I tilt the board around to let the colors flow and blend.

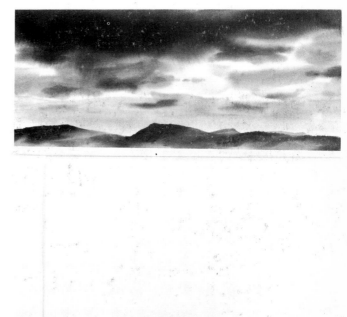

I let the sky, with its new dark clouds, dry.

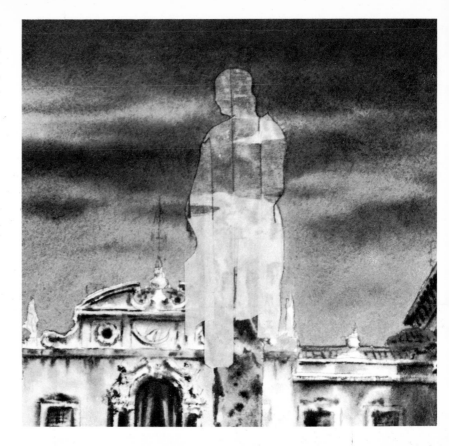

(Right) Before I add dark clouds to the sky of Vizcaya, I cover the statue with masking tape, extending the tape into the sky area. Then I cut through the tape along the outline of the statue with an X-Acto knife blade and remove the tape outside the outline.

(Below) When I've washed in the darker values in the sky, I carefully peel the tape off the statue, and the painting is complete.

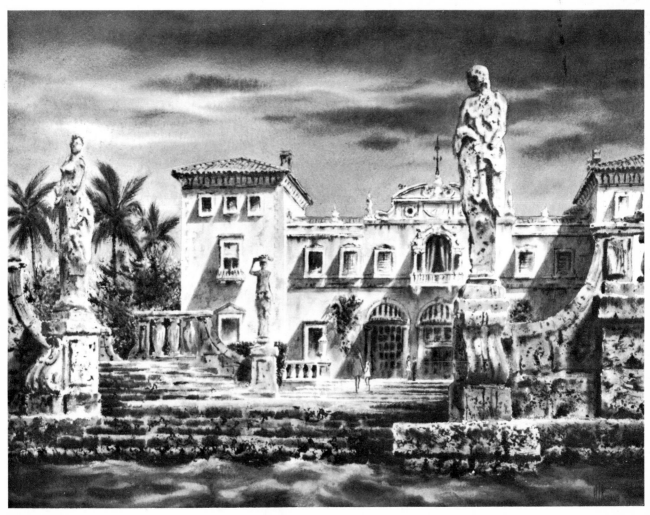

er rhythm, giving the whole picture a better mood and harmony.

Finally, I use sandpaper occasionally to remove original sky washes after they've dried too dark. I use this method only as a last resort, in a final effort to salvage a painting—not as a handy remedy when something goes wrong! I simply sand the original washes off the paper, using medium and then fine sandpaper. As it removes the pigment, the sandpaper takes the texture of the paper with it and leaves the surface soft and smooth. Then, I re-wet the paper and apply new washes. When these settle and dry on the smooth paper, the granular effect of the paint particles is quite different from the effect created on rough paper. Although I've used this method successfully to remove small areas of sky, I'd feel safer using it in foregrounds, bushes, trees, mountains, and buildings, where I can soften edges, stipple, and spatter to hide the effects of the sandpaper. In the following illustrations, I've done a "test run" of a large sky area, to show you how this method works. I used 300 lb. Arches paper—anything lighter would not stand up to the rough treatment.

Altering Foregrounds

To decide why a foreground doesn't seem to function properly, examine the painting closely and ask your-self whether the foreground is too dark, too light, too sparse, too busy, or not busy enough. I've altered foregrounds for all of these reasons.

Occasionally, when a finished painting seems unsuccessful to me, I realize that the foreground isn't heavy enough—that it's too light in value or too thin in feeling—or that it "jumps out" and detracts from the more important elements of the painting. At these times, I simply mix up some thick, deep color and proceed to paint and drybrush directly over the existing foreground to deepen it, so the viewer's eye can "sail" right over this area to the lighter and more exciting elements.

There are other occasions when I really don't know why the foreground doesn't work. (Looking at the picture in a mirror can give you a fresh perspective at times like this.) I've removed and repainted foregrounds as many as four or five times before something subtle happens to make the picture work.

Sometimes, when I have a deadline to meet and no time to "digest" the picture, I place the entire painting under a floodlight and use a piece of cardboard to cast a shadow over part, or all, of the foreground. This helps me decide whether I should darken the foreground (or other areas of the painting) by overpainting, or come to the conclusion that I should lighten it by sponging it out almost completely and repainting.

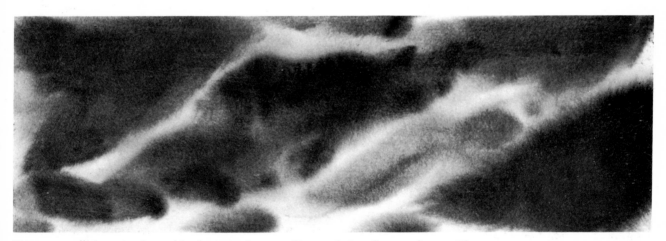

To remove all the paint from this sky area, I use medium and then fine sandpaper. The sandpaper removes some of the paper's texture as it removes the pigment.

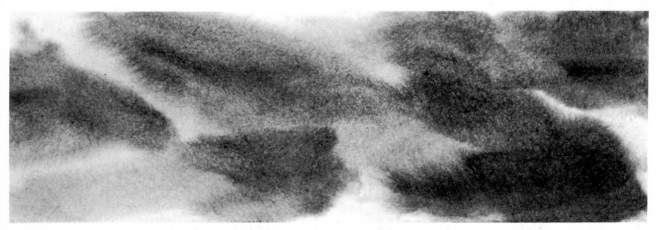

The sanded paper is now white again—and smooth. I rewet it and apply my new sky washes.

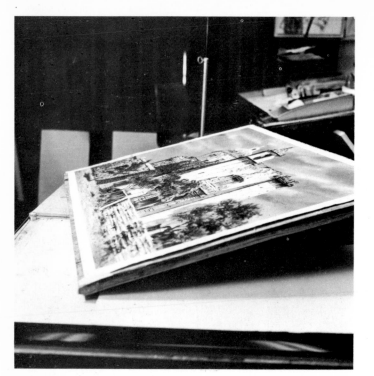

To improve this painting, I consider darkening the fore-ground. Before I actually add darker colors to the painting, I'll throw a cast shadow on the area to see if this makes an improvement.

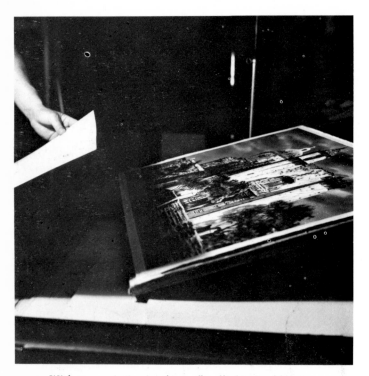

With my painting under a floodlight, I add a temporary cast shadow by holding a piece of cardboard in front of the painting. If I like this darker effect, I'll darken the fore-ground or some other areas of the painting.

In *Pennsylvania Farm*, I painted and repainted the bottom left side of the foreground before I was satisfied with it. Then the small hill didn't seem right —either the color was good and the value was off, or the value was too deep and muddy—so I decided to correct it. I painted directly over the foreground, but to no avail. Then I sponged out half the foreground and repainted it twice more before I finally arrived at the picture you see here. Just before the area was completely dry, I gave it a light spatter treatment. Remember that spatter, too, can revive a dull wash by adding texture and excitement.

Adding New Elements

Sometimes, you can correct a painting that doesn't seem to work by simply injecting a new element. But *don't* make any snap decisions and start adding things to the painting itself! Your idea may be exciting, but it may be dead wrong for the picture. Instead, try out your new element—a tree, shadow, fence, etc.—on an acetate overlay.

Tape a large piece of prepared acetate to the top of the picture so you can lift it up a easily as you com-pare your new design with your original painting. (Paint won't adhere to regular acetate, but you can buy commercially prepared acetate with a surface that's rough enough for the paint to cling to.) Then simply paint the new design and see how it fits. Think about it for awhile, consider moving it around, and try living with it on acetate for a few days before you make your final commitment.

I've done this many times; I've even "tried out" new elements on paintings that were already framed by painting on the glass with opaque colors! It's also a handy technique you can use to help you decide whether or not to alter a sky or foreground.

When you decide to add your new element, your next question is how to "bring back" the white paper. Although masking and sponging-out works fairly well in large areas, this method doesn't leave the paper really white. Since your new design element will probably be rather small, I suggest you scrape out its shape by first removing most of the original pigment and the top layer of paper with an X-Acto knife blade, then burnishing the exposed paper with an electric eraser. The blade leaves the surface of the paper in a rough state, and your washes will look much better if you smooth the area with the electric eraser before you apply them.

In *Old House in St. Augustine, Florida*, the fore-ground never pleased me. After I sponged it out and repainted it three times, I decided to add some new forms to the composition. The idea of inserting an-other tree into the picture grabbed me, so I drew in and scraped out the shape of the tall tree on the right with a blade and then smoothed the white paper with my electric eraser. I rendered the tree with touches of color, gently wet the sky around it, and added the Spanish moss. Then I decided that still another object was necessary in the already crowded composition, so I drew the outline of a boat directly over the bushes in the foreground, scraped out the paint, erased, and

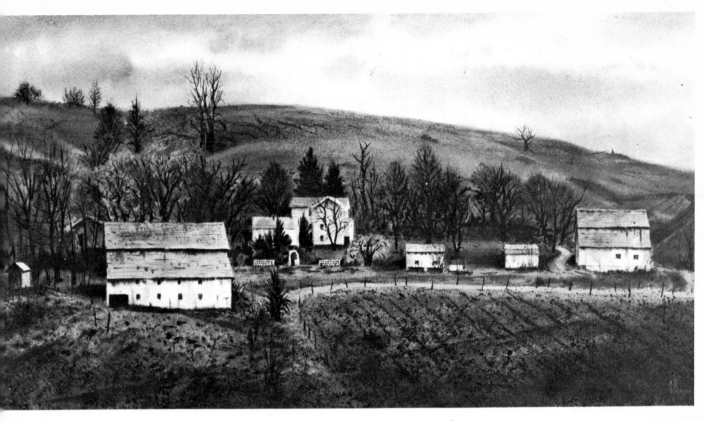

I repainted the bottom left area of the foreground in Pennsylvania Farm, *tried more corrections, then sponged it out and repainted twice more before I was satisfied. Before the final attempt was dry, I spattered some dark color on the foreground.*

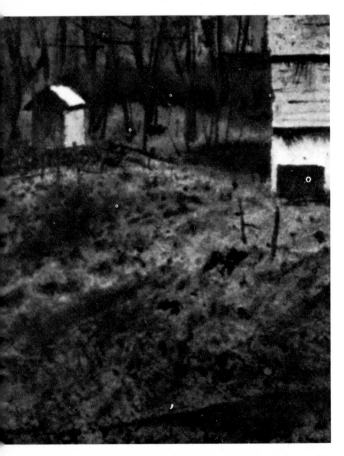

The spatter in this foreground—my final touch—adds texture and excitement to the area.

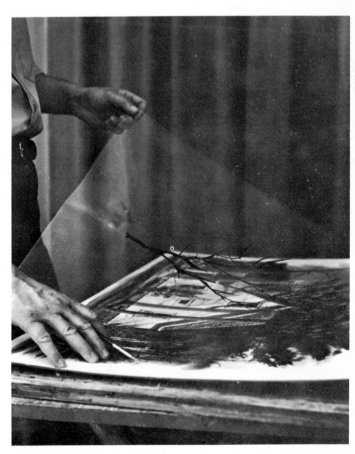

Before I add a new element directly to a painting, I try it out on an overlay of prepared acetate.

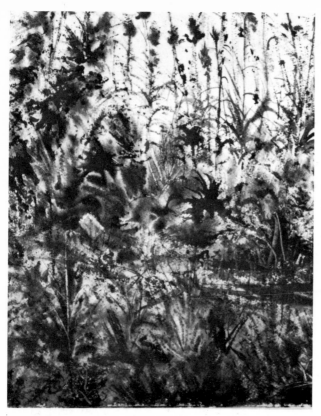

I want to add a new element—a piece of newspaper—to the dark center area of this painting. To do this, I have to first "bring back" the white paper underneath.

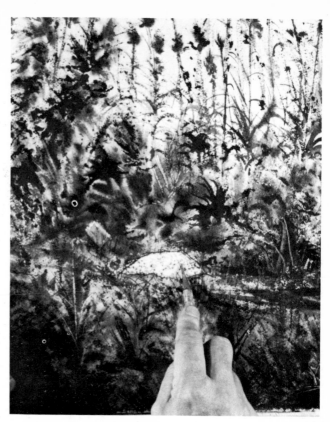

I remove the original pigment by scraping it off with an X-Acto knife blade, which leaves the surface of the paper rather rough.

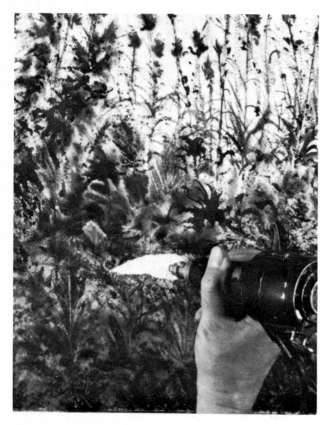

To smooth the paper where the blade has scratched it, I burnish it with an electric eraser.

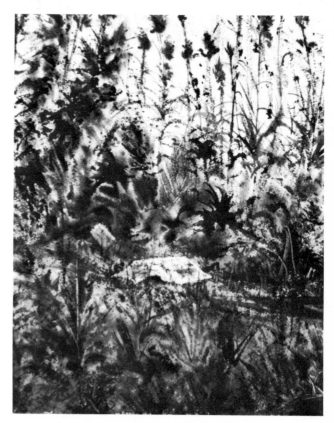

On the "new" white paper, I paint the piece of newspaper, giving better balance to the composition.

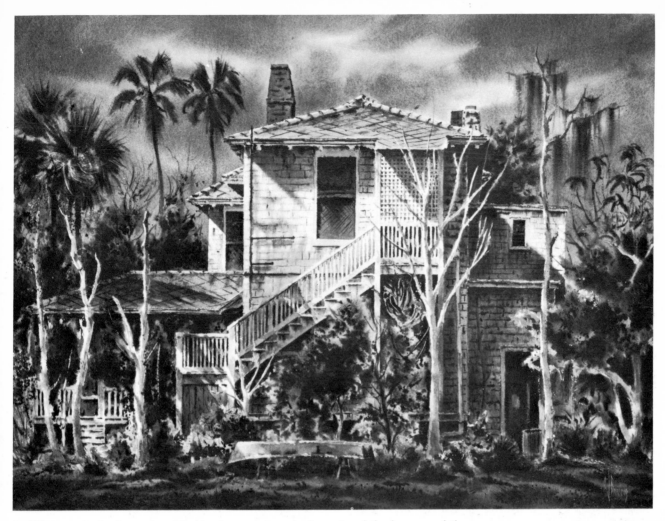

In Old House in St. Augustine, Florida, *I sponged out and repainted the foreground three times before I decided to add another tree and the boat.*

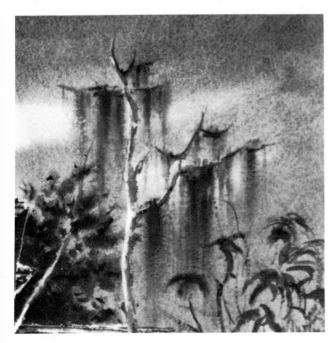

I scraped out the shape of the tall tree on the right with a blade and then burnished the paper with my electric eraser. Then I rendered the tree and added the Spanish moss wet-in-wet.

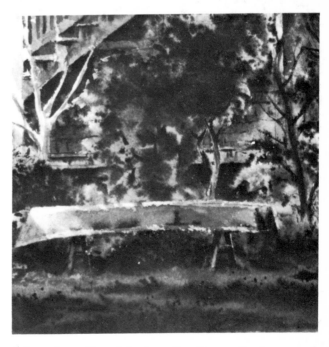

I drew the outline of the boat directly over the foreground, then scraped out the paint, burnished, and painted in the boat and shadows.

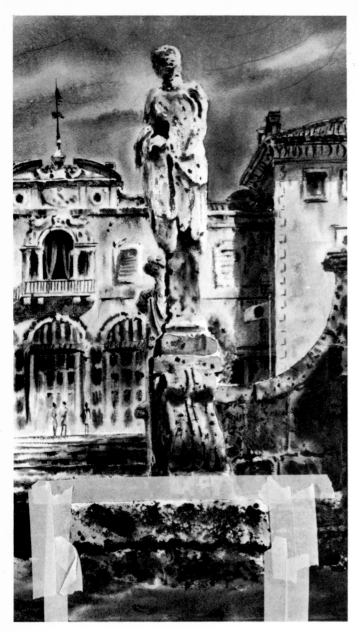

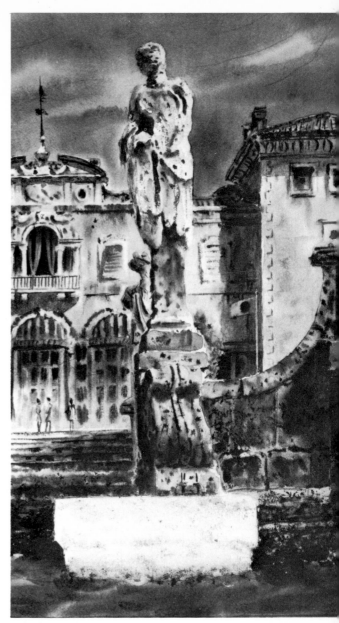

In Vizcaya, I wanted to correct small details on the base of the statue, so I surrounded the area with masking tape and sponged out the washes inside.

I removed the tape, and the base of the statue was ready to be repainted.

painted in the boat and shadows. This will give you some idea of the changes you can make in a "finished" painting if you decide they're absolutely necessary.

Correcting Small Details

In small areas, the method of scraping and erasing I just described works fairly well; you can also use the sponging out technique to correct small details.

For example, in the first illustration of *Vizcaya,* you can see that I surrounded the base of the statue with masking tape. Then I sponged out the entire base with a natural sponge and clear water and let the area dry. In the second illustration, I've lifted off the tape and I'm ready to rework the area. Although the paper wasn't quite as white as it was originally, it was certainly good enough for the corrections I made.

BIBLIOGRAPHY

Blake, Wendon, *Acrylic Watercolor Painting.* New York: Watson-Guptill, 1970.

Brandt, Rex, *Watercolor Landscape.* New York: Reinhold, 1963.

Guptill, Arthur, *Watercolor Painting Step-by-Step.* ed. by Susan E. Meyer, New York: Watson-Guptill, 1967.

Hilder, Rowland, *Starting with Watercolour.* New York: Watson-Guptill, 1967. London: Studio Vista, 1967.

Kautzky, Ted, *Painting Trees and Landscape in Watercolor.* New York and London: Reinhold, 1952.

Kent, Norman, *100 Watercolor Techniques.* ed. by Susan E. Meyer, New York: Watson-Guptill, 1968.

O'Hara, Eliot, *Watercolor with O'Hara.* New York: Putnam, 1965.

Olsen, Herb, *Watercolor Made Easy.* New York and London: Reinhold, 1955.

Pellew, John C., *Painting in Watercolor.* New York: Watson-Guptill, 1970.

Pike, John, *Watercolor.* New York: Watson-Guptill, 1966.

Richmond, Leonard, and Littlejohns, J., *Fundamentals of Watercolor Painting.* New York: Watson-Guptill, 1970.

Szabo, Zoltan, *Landscape Painting in Watercolor.* New York: Watson-Guptill, 1971.

Whitaker, Frederic, *Whitaker on Watercolor.* New York and London: Reinhold, 1963.

Whitney, Edgar A., *Complete Guide to Watercolor Painting.* New York: Watson-Guptill, 1965.

INDEX

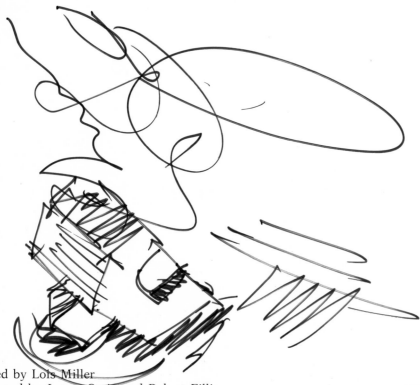

Edited by Lois Miller
Designed by James Craig and Robert Fillie
Set in 10 point Astro by University Graphics, Inc.
Printed and bound in Japan by Toppan Printing Company Ltd.